J. SIDLOW BAXTER
A HEART AWAKE

J. Sidlow Baxter
A Heart Awake

The Authorized Biography

E. A. Johnston

BakerBooks
Grand Rapids, Michigan

© 2005 by E. A. Johnston

Published by Baker Books
a division of Baker Publishing Group
P.O. Box 6287, Grand Rapids, MI 49516-6287
www.bakerbooks.com

Printed in the United States of America

Library of Congress Cataloging-in-Publication Data
Johnston, E. A. (Ernest A.)
    J. Sidlow Baxter: a heart awake : the authorized biography / E. A. Johnston.
        p.   cm.
    Includes bibliographical references.
    ISBN 0-8010-1274-0 (hardcover)
    1. Baxter, J. Sidlow (James Sidlow) I. Title: James Sidlow Baxter, a heart awake. II. Title.
BR1725.B384J64 2005
280'.4'092—dc22   2004020041

Cover photo and the same photo used on half title page by Wilbur Cadell.

Scripture is taken from the King James Version of the Bible.

Permission was granted for use of materials from the following sources:

Explore the Book One Volume Edition by J. Sidlow Baxter. Copyright © by J. Sidlow Baxter. Used by permission of The Zondervan Corporation.

The God You Should Know by J. Sidlow Baxter. Copyright © 1984 by the estate of J. Sidlow Baxter. Used by permission.

Our High Calling by J. Sidlow Baxter. Copyright © 1993 by the estate of J. Sidlow Baxter. Used by permission.

The Master Theme of the Bible by J. Sidlow Baxter. Copyright © 1997 by the estate of J. Sidlow Baxter. Used by permission.

Divine Healing of the Body by J. Sidlow Baxter. Copyright © 1979 by the estate of J. Sidlow Baxter. Used by permission.

Daily Wings by J. Sidlow Baxter. Copyright © 1983 by The Zondervan Corporation. Used by permission of The Zondervan Corporation.

Awake My Heart by J. Sidlow Baxter. Copyright © 1994 by Kregel Publications. Used by permission of the publisher.

A New Call to Holiness by J. Sidlow Baxter. Copyright © 1993 by Kregel Publications. Used by permission of the publisher.

Does God Still Guide? by J. Sidlow Baxter. Copyright © 1971 by the estate of J. Sidlow Baxter. Used by permission.

Going Deeper by J. Sidlow Baxter. Copyright © 1960 by the estate of J. Sidlow Baxter. Used by permission.

With heartfelt appreciation the following chapters
are dedicated to my dear friend,

Mrs. J. Sidlow Baxter (Isa):

few have seen such a jewel shine more brilliantly,
few have known such indomitable character.

CONTENTS

FOREWORD

I t is a pleasure and a challenge to introduce this volume on the life of the late, great J. Sidlow Baxter. In some ways he was very much like the apostle Paul—a great scholar and theologian. Yet he would have epitomized the apostle John who emphasized to us God's mighty love. Also, when I think of J. Sidlow Baxter, I think of a man upon whom the spirit of Daniel is resting. He was fearless and courageous and, like Daniel, had served the Lord from his youth up. Or could it be that J. Sidlow Baxter had the soul of a David, the sweet singer of Israel? He was not only a theologian, a preacher, and a prophet, but he was also a great musician.

Born in Australia, he was brought up in England. From his youth he had a deep love for music and became an accomplished pianist. He was converted at the age of sixteen, and by nineteen he was the National Young Life Campaign pianist. This was the largest evangelical movement in England. God used J. Sidlow Baxter as a preacher, prophet, evangelist, and musician while he was still a teenager. His was a life multifaceted and greatly used.

J. Sidlow Baxter studied for the ministry at Spurgeon's College. He served three pastorates with unusual blessing. His last pastorate was in Edinburgh, where he pastored the largest Baptist church in Scotland. After twenty years

God called him to a wider ministry. He traveled extensively, preaching, teaching, and sharing the glorious gospel of Jesus Christ.

Perhaps his greatest legacy is his written work. He was a gifted and prolific author. When booksellers wanted a book of devotions to place in the library of the president of the United States, they chose J. Sidlow Baxter's book *Awake My Heart*. It was leather bound and placed in that library so that the president might read it and be inspired.

Baxter wrote twenty-six books in all. Among the best, and the one that I want to commend especially to you, is *Explore the Book*. This comprehensive overview of the Bible is without parallel and has been studied in Bible schools and seminaries around the world.

A personal word is fitting here. I love this man like few men I have known. His intellect and devotion have strengthened my own ministry. To be around J. Sidlow Baxter was to be enriched.

Now let me say a word about the author of this volume. E. A. Johnston has labored faithfully to capture the heart and mind of J. Sidlow Baxter. He has done careful research and prayerful writing. I am grateful that he has taken this task. This volume has done much to strengthen my own life, and I believe it will be used correspondingly in the lives of many others. He has done the kingdom of God a great service by writing this volume for us. Much of what I have read in this biography is new to me; therefore, I treasure it all the more.

I encourage the reader to enjoy and absorb this volume. I don't want to sound overly enthusiastic, but I sincerely say, with all of my heart, when you read it, you will be blessed.

DR. ADRIAN ROGERS
SENIOR PASTOR
BELLEVUE BAPTIST CHURCH
MEMPHIS, TENNESSEE

ACKNOWLEDGMENTS

I first want to acknowledge my blessed Lord who is the solid rock on which I stand and the sovereign King whom I serve. I wish to thank my beautiful wife, Carla, and darling daughter, Carly, for their patience and love during my absence in writing. I must acknowledge the memory of Clem Dear of Oak Park, Illinois, who led me to the Lord in 1968. I am indebted to both Dr. Adrian Rogers, my beloved pastor, and Dr. Stephen F. Olford, my beloved mentor. The encouragement and support I have received from both these giants in the faith is deeply appreciated. [Dr. Stephen F. Olford passed away during the time the manuscript was being edited for publication.—Ed.]

I would also like to acknowledge the following: Mrs. J. Sidlow Baxter (Isa) who at age ninety-seven is my inspiration and dear, dear friend. [Mrs. Isa Baxter passed away just a few days after her ninety-eighth birthday, during the time the manuscript was being edited for publication.—Ed.] Dr. H. D. McCarty and his staff at University Baptist Church in Fayetteville, Arkansas, for their warm welcome and hospitality. Dr. Darwin and Eleanor Holian for hospitality in Santa Barbara. Satellite Music and Video in Edinburgh,

Scotland, for the many introductions to the Scottish friends of Sidlow who are still living.

I must give gratitude to Sidlow Baxter's niece, Mrs. Muriel Catt. Through her friendship and help I was able to put the early years of her Uncle Sid together; plus she provided rare family photos from her grandmother's album and wrote photo catpions for chapter 1. I further acknowledge my debt to Reverend Keith Skelton for his unwavering support, dutiful assistance, and warm friendship. Also, I express appreciation to Charlotte Chapel in Edinburgh, Spurgeon's Theological College in London, Bethesda Free Church in Sunderland, England, and Heritage College and Seminary (formerly Central Baptist Seminary) in Canada, each for the use of their archives. Also, the J. Sidlow Baxter Library in Fayetteville, Arkansas, provided the taped messages of Dr. Baxter. I am indebted to Chuck Adams of Northampton for physically going to Spurgeon's College in London for me and providing some of the best photos in the book. I must thank Sam Gordon of Trans World Radio for lugging my manuscript around Ireland. I express appreciation to Walter Cameron of Sunderland, England, for all his service in the name of the Lord. Additionally, Ian Balfour of Edinburgh for history of Charlotte Chapel.

Also, Clara Caddell of Toronto for the photos of Dr. Baxter in Canada. I was assisted by Marina Lytle on the technical aspects of my laptop.

One final thought: I wish to express my gratitude to all who participated in the chapter "The Legacy" by sending letters and emails detailing their friendship with Dr. Baxter through the years. I must not forget Dr. Vicki Crumpton at Baker Book House for believing in the project and seeing it through to publication. May the Lord bless and reward the aforementioned abundantly!

INTRODUCTION

L et me introduce you to J. Sidlow Baxter by telling some stories about my interactions with him that reveal the kind of man he was. Sidlow was a man of prayer. Whether we were kneeling in my study or at a convention with other speakers, I just wanted to hear him pray. He had a way of praying which was awesome.

He told me how he was converted. The Wood brothers began a movement across England called the Young Life Campaign. Fred Wood was an outstanding evangelist with an incredible heart. Sidlow was a get-around-town young man who was searching for truth and fascinated with detective stories. The Wood brothers had hired a theatre for a crusade in a certain town in the Midlands of England. On the marquee were the subjects for each night. This particular one was "The Infallible Detective." Sidlow saw it either in the paper or from the street and said to himself, "'The Infallible Detective,' I'm not missing that!" So, in he came. I believe that Fred Wood's preaching would have appealed to him because his sermons were well argued. The text was, "Be sure your sin will find you out." That night sin found Sidlow out, and he was converted. Now I have a sermon called "The Infallible Detective," and I've used Sidlow Baxter's story hundreds of times in crusades!

Sid and I were friends and on a number of occasions we happened to be in the same conventions and conferences. In particular, I refer to the Keswick in Port Stewart, Ireland. He was there with Donald Grey Barnhouse. He made quite an impact on Barnhouse, so much so that when he was over in the United States and Barnhouse couldn't teach at his New York Bible study class (which was always held on a Monday night), Sid would stand in for him. I just couldn't believe my eyes or ears to see and hear those two as friends: one an Arminian and the other a hard-boiled Calvinist!

On one occasion, I went to a Manhattan church to hear Sid preach. I remember there was a very high pulpit, almost like Charlotte Chapel in Edinburgh, and an incident occurred right in the middle of Sidlow's message. A tame tomcat came walking on the rails toward Sid, and, of course, all eyes looked that way. Without breaking a step, Sid said, "and that reminds me of that wonderful portion of Luke's Gospel that records *the Magnificat*." Well, the crowd went wild. It took five minutes to calm them!

He took me by surprise one time. He phoned me and said he was in town at the Hotel Salisbury, next to our church. Of course, I felt obliged and said, "Sorry I didn't know you were around or I would have asked you to preach on Sunday at Calvary." "No, my brother," he answered. "No problem. No problem. That's your throne. You guard your throne. Let nobody interfere with your throne. That's your throne."

He came to my study at the hotel and we had a long, long discussion on "everything": the two natures, the American scene, preaching, and on various other issues. Eventually I said, "It's lunchtime. I have booked a local restaurant, please come along with me." So Sid got up and grabbed his briefcase. I said, "No need for that, my brother, just leave it right in my study." "No, no, no," he said, and brought it with him. So we went down to this beautiful restaurant where you could get the best fish. We were taken to our seats, sat down, and the menus were brought. And I thought to myself, *I wonder what this man's going to eat.* So the waiter came. And I said, "Sid, go ahead. He said, "No thanks. All I want is a glass of water and maybe a pot of tea." I said, "Man alive, this is a great fish restaurant!" Well, I ordered—I had to make a quick decision—a little fish dish.

The waiter brought it and Sid said, "Let us pray. LET US PRAY." With his arms spread out he prayed. And then to my *horror*, with these swanky Yankees all around us, he opened his little briefcase and brought out his *Biblical* diet! I mean *everybody* was looking at me. I really couldn't get over it. There he was with a little bit of this, and a little bit of that, and he began to stir into the concoction the hot water he had ordered! He ate his meal while I ate my fish! That was Sidlow.

The next morning he was away again, but I remember his defending my pulpit. "That's your throne. That's your throne, let no one dethrone you." Then this incredible meal together. I normally wouldn't even go to that restaurant, it was too costly, and he ordered nothing but a pot of tea and hot water! That's why he carried his briefcase with his Biblical diet and his little containers!

He was always immaculately dressed and looked the picture of dignity every time he stood in the pulpit. He was a striking figure with that white hair. His language and flowing speech were quite a contrast to his "concoction" in a swanky restaurant!

Early in my ministry, in the UK, we were often at conventions together. One was in South Wales where he overshot his speaking time. I was the second speaker and only had about twenty minutes, and for some reason or another the conveners insisted we keep to the time allotted, so that I had to curtail my message. Another occasion we were together and he was the second speaker and the first speaker took *his* time. I remember Sid got up and said, "My brother, and the message he has brought, reminds me of a conference to which two of our preachers went, and the first man started with *condemnation*, then went on to *justification*, and then *sanctification*, and then *glorification*." Then he said, "Now I must go to the *station*, so I can't preach anymore." He had the crowd roaring.

Then we were together at the Port Stewart convention, in Ireland, and whom should we be once more yoked with than Dr. Donald Barnhouse. Dr. Barnhouse opened the convention with a complicated address on Ephesians and likened it to the tabernacle with its outer court, the Holy Place, the Holy of Holies, and so forth. Then followed Sidlow Baxter. I don't know whether he dropped his bag or handed it to his driver, but he didn't have a Bible! So, he borrowed a Gideon Bible. He opened it to the Ephesians epistle. I don't know whether or not he did it for effect, because Sid was quite an actor, but he bellowed forth, "Well now! How interesting! God led my brother to speak on Ephesians and here I am determined to speak on Ephesians. But first of all let's examine what my brother Donald's been talking about. He calls Ephesians the picture of the tabernacle. I think it is more like a BARNHOUSE!" The crowd roared!

But somehow he reconciled the whole issue with his incredible winsomeness; then what he did was not the Barnhouse approach, because Barnhouse was not a homiletician. He was more of a theologian who went into the Greek words and so on. I mean, Barnhouse could preach a whole message on one word, and with his Ph.D. researchers, he could fill a book with one word. So, Barnhouse went one way with the message and Sid opened up Ephesians and gave the

16

divisions, all with brilliant expositions. I can't remember a single thing Barnhouse said apart from that one opening address. But Sidlow's treatment of Ephesians throughout that week at Port Stewart Keswick Convention remains with me to this day.

When Sid finished with a subject it was sheer clarity and finality. You didn't see how he could add anything to it. And in that sense, he seemed to be a reproduction of Graham Scroggie. Dr. Graham Scroggie's ministry was obviously followed and studied by Sidlow Baxter. They were similar in structure, homiletics, and to a certain extent, good use of alliteration.

Now, Sidlow had a creative mind. When he couldn't find a word that fit, he just coined one and used it with ease! He also loved to delve into areas that could be termed controversial. And when we met at conventions he would come up to me and say, "Oh my Stephen. Oh my Stephen. My Stephen." We were very fond of each other. At one time I had all his books, and hopefully one day we'll get all his books back again for our library here.

Dr. Stephen F. Olford, founder
The Stephen Olford Center for Biblical Preaching
Memphis, Tennessee

one

|||||||||||||||||||||||||||||||||||||||||||||||||||||||||||||||||||||||||||||||||||||

THE LAD

Now Samuel did not yet know the LORD, neither was the word of the LORD yet revealed unto him. And the LORD called Samuel again the third time. And he arose and went to Eli, and said, Here am I; for thou didst call me. And Eli perceived that the LORD had called the child.

1 SAMUEL 3:7–8

His Birth

What youthful mind has not wistfully daydreamed of olde England? With its colorful lore of castles and knights, kings and queens, its empire could make nations quake. England's scepter stretched across the globe, its Royal Navy ruled the seas, and nations' leaders bowed to her throne.

So it was to England that Alice Baxter returned, without her unfaithful husband, John, leaving behind in Australia the turbulent memories of her troubled marriage and taking with her their three small children and her faith in God. Little Sid was two at the time.

Although James Sidlow Baxter was born February 25, 1903, in Sydney, Australia, it would be the green hills and rolling countryside of England he would remember. The Pennine Hills of Ashton-under-Lyne in Lancashire, England, welcomed the Baxter family with smiling peaks. He would grow up to treasure the memory of those Pennine Hills, for they represented the delights of his youth. He grew up playing in their valleys, he sought refuge in their majesty, and as he grew up in their shadow he discovered the beauty of love and the discouragements of life.

He and sisters Daisy and Eunice would frolic in the flower-speckled meadows unaware of the poverty and hardship of a single mother raising three children in a mill town. Life was hard for most people in those earlier times in England. The workday began well before dawn and ended after sunset. People labored in fields and factories earning their bread with the sweat from their brow. It was a time before world wars. It was a time before televisions and computers. It was a time now forgotten. But it was also a time that J. Sidlow Baxter would fondly recall for the rest of his life.

His Mother

> And extol God above for the gift of her love!
> The debt that I owe I can never know
> There's no one just like her, that mother of mine.
>
> JSB

Alice Baxter was a hardworking Christian woman who loved her Lord as much as she loved her three young children. Daisy, Eunice, and Sidlow were the joy that sustained

20

The Baxter Family. **Back row:** Oswald Baines and Eunice Isabella Baines (brother-in-law and sister); James Sidlow Baxter; Margaret Alice Baxter (Daisy; sister); **Front row:** Alice Baxter (mother); John Baxter (father). Taken around 1922. (Photos and captions in this chapter courtesy of Mrs. Muriel Catt, daughter of Oswald and Eunice Baines and niece of J. Sidlow Baxter.)

her during those difficult early years. It was Alice's faith in the Lord Jesus and her devoted service to him that made her a well-respected citizen in that little town in Lancashire County.

For twenty years she was the police court missionary. She was the one who gave a hand up to the down-and-out. Her work in the rescue missions was hard, and at times discouraging, although the children never heard her complain. Her efforts in the rescue missions so impressed young Sidlow that when he died almost a hundred years later he bequeathed all his clothing to the local rescue mission in the city of Santa Barbara, California.

Alice canvassed the environs of Manchester. She walked everywhere wearing her blue uniform and blue bonnet, visiting the women prisoners at the jail, then going door-to-door in the slum areas of town to hand out gospel tracts. She trusted in the power of Christ to transform a person's

John Baxter, Sid's father

character no matter how bad that person was. She never believed in social reform and its assumption that a better environment led to better citizens. She believed that communal problems stemmed from a moral and spiritual vacuum that only the gospel of Christ could transform.

At the evening meal table Alice would share the day's "case histories" with the three children—a young trinity is the term Sid used to describe him and his siblings. Their eager minds would listen in suspense to the lurid tales of some

Sid's grandmother and stepgrandfather Clough

poor woman in prison who was the victim of her own descent into sin. It usually began with a casual sip of beer "just to be social," then the poor girl would take that liquid gateway to dirty sex and eventual ruin in a life mired in pig swill. The downgrade was always the same: liquor, sex, and ruin. These tales of horribly ruined individuals so scared young Sid that he lived a pure life from then on. He did not want to end up in prison or in pig swill.

Occasionally, some of these ruined women would accept the gospel message that Alice shared with them, and their lives would be transformed to the glory of God. Alice loved to tell the children those stories of victory over sin.

Yet it was her dedication to the Lord's service that stuck out in Sid's mind many years later. One such incident he relates in his book *Does God Still Guide?*:

My beloved mother was out delivering Gospel tracts in a slummy city area. She prayed that each tract might find the right target. She knocked at a door, and waited. No one answered, but she heard movement within, so she knocked again. After three knocks and waits the door slowly opened, and a rough-faced man was there, on hands and knees, or, rather, on hands and stumps—for both legs had been amputated above the knees, as a result of a recent accident. My mother immediately apologized for having brought him to the door, but he did not mind, and was willing enough to take the tract. He gave one glance at it, and then, with quivering lips, asked, "Missis, did you pick this one specially for me?" The title of the tract was: NOT A LEG TO STAND UPON!—and it was used of God to bring home to the man his spiritual condition before God.[1]

J. Sidlow Baxter fondly spoke of his mother throughout his life. She was the compass that guided him through life's troubled waters. She was the godly influence that molded him. And her many prayers for him shaped his character and taught him to lean on an almighty God in every circumstance of life.

When young Sid turned sixteen, Alice handed her son a Bible with the inscription, "'Whatsoever he saith unto you, do it.' John 2:5." It was the text of Jesus' mother Mary telling the servants at the wedding to prepare the water pots of stone for the first miracle of Jesus turning water into wine. Years later, Sid realized the magnitude of that verse for his life. He later commented, "It was years before my thick head realized that my dear mother was telling me that whatsoever Jesus saith unto *me* to do it!"

Another example of her godly influence in his life occurred when a teenage Sid was at a movie theater with some friends watching a Buster Keaton comedy. Everyone in the theater was laughing except Sid. He felt uneasy, so he left the theater and ventured out in the rain and walked home. As he approached the door he heard a voice inside. At first he thought it belonged to a nosy neighbor whom he disliked so he turned to walk away. But then, recognizing the voice to be that of his mother, he stopped to listen and peeked through the window. There on the hard wooden floor was Alice, on her knees, praying audibly, "Oh Lord Jesus, wherever my dear son Sid is tonight in your world, I pray that you make him uneasy so he will not enjoy it." The young J. Sidlow Baxter quietly turned in the doorway and walked back out into the rain. As cold pellets of rain hit the back of Sid's neck, he pulled his coat collar up to lessen the sting as he walked away from the little cottage where his mother remained, interceding with God for her rebellious son.

Alice Baxter, Sid's Mother

His Childhood

The weather in England, seldom friendly, is cruelest in winter. It was December 1908. Sidlow was age five. In the typical working-class cottage of that era, heating was limited to a single fireplace of the living room downstairs. Coal was a precious commodity.

It was a December they each would remember. Little Sidlow had the measles. He was trembling and cold—he could not stay warm. The local doctor advised Alice to bring his bed downstairs into the warm room. Over Christmas the little boy worsened. The frail laddie's resistance was low and the measles turned into whooping cough. Coughing spasms wrecked havoc on his little frame. Then the worst happened. The dreaded illness that seizes the weakened—lobar pneumonia—set in. The following days were terrifying for the family.

Daisy and Eunice were sent to Rostherne to stay with relatives lest they come down ill as well. The doctor visited their cottage to examine the frail, feverish patient. The physician's countenance was grim and he had bad news for Alice. He felt Sid would not make it to the morning for meningitis had now set in. He advised the young mother to prepare for the worst.

Alice did the only thing a godly mother could do—she prayed. All through the night she cried out to God for mercy for her little Sid. She reminded God of the covenant she had made with him, whereby she had set her boy apart for the ministry of the gospel. She pleaded for God to spare him so that the boy could grow up to tell others about Jesus Christ. Finally, somewhere through her tears and intercession, the Lord gave her a verse to stand upon. It was in Psalm 30:5: "Weeping may endure for a night, But joy cometh in the morning."

The next morning the doctor arrived, expecting the worst. To his surprise the little patient smiled as he entered the room. It was a miracle, he said; young Sid was healed. Alice bid farewell to the doctor and shut the door. Then she got on her knees to give thanks and praise to the Almighty One who had heard her prayer.

It was not to be the last time J. Sidlow Baxter would come close to death and be healed. God had a very special purpose and plan for Sid and God remembers his covenants with his people.

Baxter speaks of another pivotal childhood incident in his devotional book *Daily Wings*:

> When I was five I went with my mother to an evangelistic meeting. After preaching, the missioner gave the "invitation"

and I was one of several who went out across a corridor to anterooms where counselors waited to help us. The lady who dealt with me was a near neighbor. With wonderful diplomacy she said, "Oh Sid, how delighted we are to see you coming to receive Jesus!" To a five-year-old that meant much. The text she used was Revelation 3:20, "Behold, I stand at the door, and knock! If any man hear my voice, and open the door, I will come in . . ." Afterward I went back to the main hall, to an addendum meeting in which testimonies were being given. When a pause came I stood, and my little voice piped out, "Tonight I have taken Jesus as my Savior, and such a burden has rolled away . . ." I got no further. Sitting in front of my mother and me were two maiden ladies, one of whom loudly whispered, "How ridiculous! A mere child talking like that!" My mind went confused. My cheeks crimsoned. I faltered and sank down humiliated. This conversion business suddenly seemed an adult sham. From then onward I just could not believe. I shut Jesus out of my life, and grew up a thorough worldling. Oh, how careful we should be with children! How harmed they can be by thoughtless comment![2]

Those cruel words drove a dagger into his little heart and the wounded boy would remain a worldling well into his midteens. God would eventually heal Sid's wounded heart—as he heals all wounded hearts that turn to him.

His Youth

England during J. Sidlow Baxter's youth is best explained by his own words from his book *For God So Loved,*

When I was a young boy over in England, the British empire was at its zenith, with a population of four hundred and ten million, embracing twelve and one-half million square

miles, one fifth of the world's surface and over one-fifth of
its inhabitants; the widest-spreading empire ever known. At
that time a common saying was, "All roads lead to London,"
greatest city on earth and metropolis of the largest empire
ever. All the main railroads and all the main roadways led
to London. All the main sea-routes seemed directly or in-
directly connected to London. It was a resounding echo of
the long-ago cry, "All roads lead to Rome."[3]

Growing up in England made his constitution hearty. Over-
coming the earlier illness that almost killed him, he grew strong
in the inclement weather and his physical frame filled out to
his tall stature. Now a normal healthy lad, he enjoyed the sports
of youth. With his schoolmates he played football and enjoyed
learning the sport of boxing. Bullies learned to respect his fists.
Yet, for all his budding manliness, Sidlow had a more tender
side to him which blossomed in the arts. He learned to play
the piano and had a natural gift for music, even composing
hymns later in life. He possessed a poet's heart. Poetry would
be a lifelong expression for his creative talents.

Although he was a normal healthy child, one important
feature remained absent from his life: his desire for the things
of God. Alice noticed this too keenly. She continued to pray
for her strapping son, and he obediently accompanied her
to the Methodist meetings. However, all the religion in the
world could not overcome the damaging words spoken by
the two old biddies who questioned his young salvation.
He grew in stature only. His spirituality remained stagnant,
stowed away in a trampled heart.

Yet there were incidents that reminded him of a loving
God. In his book *Does God Still Guide?* he talks about such
an occurrence:

One day, away back in my youth, I was in a hen-run belong-
ing to a friend of mine. Suspended in a string-bag from
the branch of a tree was some edible substance which was

28

evidently very tasty to the hens, for they kept jumping up and pecking at it, one after another. When I asked my friend why he kept it tantalizingly hanging above them instead of on the ground, he laughed. "It's put there for a purpose," he said. "These little hens of mine need exercise, and that's one way of making sure that they get it." I have never forgotten it. How often we wonder why something dearly wanted or keenly needed seems kept just beyond our reach! Little do we realize God's good purpose in this. What spiritual exercise it causes! How it develops us in our Christian life! It often means that as well as guiding us, God is training us.[4]

Little did the youthful Sidlow know how much his heavenly Father was training him for future work. Because his tender heart had been so cruelly hurt, God seemed to be gently reminding Sid of his existence in every aspect of life. God seemed to be saying to his young heart, "For I the LORD thy God will hold thy right hand, saying unto thee, Fear not; I will help thee" (Isa. 41:13).

His Conversion

"If I may refer to my boyhood days again," Dr. Baxter writes in *Going Deeper*, "I remember how, again and again, my dear mother would softly sing the following verse before going out to her preaching appointments:

> Oh, to be nothing, nothing,
>   Simply to lie at Thy feet;
> A broken and emptied vessel
>   For my Master's use made meet!
> Emptied, that Thou mayest fill me,
>   As forth to Thy service I go;
> Emptied, that so, unhindered
> Thy life through mine might flow."[5]

Later in life, when he treasured time with Christ from waking moments to evening hours, J. Sidlow Baxter would always regret the years he spent as a "Godless worldling." He regretted those years of his youth when, instead of putting God first in his life, he had not even put him last; he had left him out altogether. He also recalled the words of his mother when asked what was the greatest commandment. She replied, "Thou shalt love the Lord thy God with all thy heart, and with all thy soul, and with all thy mind" (Matt. 22:37). He knew full well he had not been doing that.

He did not want God to interfere with his life; he had chosen his own way. He was a bright student. Handsome. The girls liked him. His fellow athletes admired him. He felt he did not need God. Yet, try as he might, Sid could not outrun God. There was the daily witness of his mother, who prayed and sang hymns around the house. There was the preaching at the Methodist church that he still attended out of respect for his mother. His intellect was telling him he was fine without God; his heart was telling him otherwise.

What impact the printed sermons (two thousand in all) of Charles H. Spurgeon have had on eternity only the courts of heaven know. Prisoners in foreign lands, getting their hands on a sermon of Spurgeon, would read and be converted to Christianity. Called the "Prince of Preachers," Spurgeon filled the five-thousand-seat Metropolitan Tabernacle in London every week until his death in 1892. And it was one of these printed sermons that fell into the hands of young Sid that would radically change his life.

One evening, while sitting up in bed, Sid was reading a sermon of Spurgeon. Sid had been taught since childhood the truths of the Bible, but they had lain dormant in his mind, producing no fruit. As he read about Christ's work on the cross and how Jesus died for him—that sin was a hereditary condition and that religion in itself never

Rev. J. Sidlow Baxter

saved a soul—suddenly a light broke forth in his mind. He saw spiritual truths he had never before realized. It wasn't long after that evening when the sixteen-year-old gave his life to Christ. He came to trust in Jesus as his Lord and

31

Savior while attending an evangelistic campaign that was conducted by Frederick and Arthur Wood, founders of the National Young Life Campaign in Britain. He would eventually join the Young Life Campaign as the touring piano player.

In his book *The Master Theme of the Bible*, he talks about that turning point in his life.

> I could not easily put into words what it meant to me when the bigger, pretemporal, preterrestrial, supercosmic meanings of the Cross really broke through into my own thinking. It gave a new poise of reassurance to my mind that nothing since, either outward or inward, has disturbed.
>
> Everything began to look different. God and the universe, time and history, permitted sin and suffering, the future of our world, and destiny beyond the grave all took on a new complexion. It did not suddenly answer all the interim questions relating to permitted troubles, and injustices now, but it utterly answered that deep-down question beneath all others as to the integrity and safety and beneficence of the universe—and of God. Problems of providence, painful enigmas, poignant puzzles of permitted injustice, and other mysteries still remained, but now I saw the light of that guaranteeing Cross streaming with prophetic promise through them all. In William Cowper's words, behind every "frowning providence" there was the "smiling face" of temporarily hidden good purpose. Through every dark cloud I saw that gleaming rainbow of evangelical covenant which overarches the throne of grace.
>
> With deepening adoration I began to discern more surely that in a way that only the crimson of Calvary could express it, God had given himself not only for me, but to me, if my loving trust would have him! I began to see, in Calvary's boundless dimensions and unobliterable guarantee, the love that would never give me up and never let me go. All fear became inexcusable, except the fear of grieving such a God,

who had now made me so willingly his again, and himself so dearly mine. It set my heart singing with richer gratitude, Wade Robinson's words:

> Heav'n above is softer blue,
> Earth around is sweeter green;
> Something lives in ev'ry hue
> Christless eyes have never seen!
> Birds with gladder songs o'erflow,
> Flow'rs with deeper beauties shine,
> Since I know, as now I know,
> I am His, and He is mine.[6]

Sidlow's life was changing. He was singing a new song. His mother's heart had never been gladder.

two

THE YOUNG ADULT

O God, thou hast taught me from my youth: and hitherto
have I declared thy wondrous works.

PSALM 71:17

His Many Talents

One cannot fathom why the Creator bestows talent and
genius overabundantly to one creature and withholds from
another. Why he blesses and overloads creative ability in
one person and seemingly bypasses another.

Why was Mozart given so much? How can one describe
the soft touch of Monet or the pain-filled brushstrokes of Van
Gogh? God-given ability falls at times into the hands of some
who cannot handle its greatness; the talent is squandered, like
Hemingway and Faulkner, or dissipated, like Flaubert and
Fitzgerald—one wonders at the potential that lay in ruin.

Yet, at times, the heavenly blessings fall upon some whose shoulders can bear them. And those that uphold the blessing honor God. We see it in the beauty of Michelangelo, the boldness of Luther, the tireless dedication of the Wesley brothers.

Occasionally, talent turns into greatness. Then, at other times, it stumbles, falters, flounders—too great of a burden and too heavy a weight to carry. Ultimately it boils down to the person on whom it falls upon, to the person's character or lack of it. Upon the slender shoulders of J. Sidlow Baxter God bestowed much. He knew he had a steward who could bear them, and bear them humbly. Until the day Sid died he was humble and honored to be so favored by God. Perhaps the secret of successful talent bearing lies within the recesses of one's humility.

Sidlow possessed many gifts from above. He could preach like a prophet. He was a wonderful writer. His novel *The Hidden Hand* is proof of his talent. He was a poet on a grand scale. He was a hymnodist who believed in keeping the tradition of hymns. He was also a first-class musician. His love for the piano would be lifelong.

In fact, Alice herself had useful ability at the piano. Back in those days, in a poor Lancashire cotton town, not many families could afford the luxury of a piano. However, Alice was able to find an old Cramer piano of which Sid said its performance was at least tolerable. Alice always said that Sid could do anything with a piano: By the time he was thirteen he had mastered Clementi's first book of sonatinas.

Sidlow also loved to read and write poetry. But music was his first love and it would continue to play a large part throughout his life. Early on he pursued music as a career. When an opportunity arose for him to become the pianist to the National Young Life Campaign in Britain, he jumped at the chance. He traveled around different cities playing the piano while another man preached a gospel message. He recounts one such occasion in his book *Majesty, The God You Should Know.*

> I recall a strange incident in those same youthful days, when I was pianist to the National Young Life Campaign in Britain. We were holding a campaign in a new civic hall which seated five thousand, in an English city. The "feel" of the meetings was good until the second Saturday night, when the atmosphere suddenly changed—for a strange reason which we did not understand at first. It was just as though, all around us, there were invisible forces of evil struggling to defeat what we were trying to do in our evangelistic gathering. Lest you should think me over-imaginative, let me say that every Christian in the building felt likewise. It was oppressive. The hymns dragged, and the choral pieces fell flat. After struggling through his evangelistic address and seemingly futile appeal, Frederick P. Wood, the preacher, sank down exhausted like a defeated wrestler.
>
> But why? Well, the reason was downstairs! Underneath the main hall where we held our meeting was a large but lesser hall in which a dance was in progress until after midnight. It was a godless voluptuous affair, with drinking and unchaste "goings on." Whether the atmosphere of our meeting got down there I doubt, but their atmosphere certainly rose to where we were! Every now and then, when certain doors swung open we could hear the blare of the jazz, and the thud, thud, thud of the big drum; and the odor of beer would somehow waft itself upstairs. It is not extra-sensory perception running wild when I say that it seemed as though a horde of invisible demon-personalities were sweeping up and violently objecting to our presence in the building. I have never forgotten it, nor ever will. It was an eye-opener to me, a young Christian, as to the utter hostility of holiness and evil.[1]

However, Sidlow's musical career was coming to a close. One morning, with the Pennine Range beside him, he walked at the break of day communing with his Lord. God's voice spoke to his heart, "Sid, Sid. Give it all to me, Sid." These words were a resounding echo that would follow him again and again in his life. Though Sid had other plans for himself—God had something in store for him that the young man did not yet know. It was as if the text from Jeremiah was directing, "Call unto me, and I will answer thee, and shew thee great and mighty things, which thou knowest not" (Jer. 33:3). At the age of nineteen he felt the call of God to preach the glad tidings of salvation to a hungry world. And it was his obedience and yielding to the Holy Spirit that would eventually surround him with success. The Lord God Jehovah would anoint the young man with an unction that would stir the spirit of a restless world and give peace to those individuals who heard J. Sidlow Baxter proclaim the Good News of salvation.

His Call to Preach

Of the many-faceted gifts of J. Sidlow Baxter, the most prominent was preaching. They called him "The Boy Preacher," for at an early age he could hold an audience spellbound while he expounded God's Word. He was eloquent and possessed a natural, self-effacing charm. Word began to spread around England of his talents in the pulpit.

However, preaching as an occupation was not his desire. He had not wanted to become a minister full-time—it was fun to preach here and there but not for the rest of his days! He had other plans for his life. Yet, on the Pennine Hills that particular morn, he had heard God's call to preach. As he read his Bible later that day, the Word of God in

1 Timothy 4:11–16 confirmed it, and it was then that the young man answered the call.

> My own decision to train for the full-time Christian ministry, was finalized in that very way. I had not wanted to be a minister, yet in my own little way I had entered into Paul's "Woe unto me if I preach not the Gospel!" I felt an inward constraint to give myself wholly to public Bible teaching. Certain circumstances, also, seemed to slant that way. Yet I was not sure. Self-aims in other directions occasioned much wrestling for a while, until I got to the place where I was reading 1 Timothy 4:11–16 (I was nineteen at the time), the completive guidance flashed into my yielded mind just when I was not particularly looking for it, and took me by surprise. So luminous and compelling did verses 15 and 16 become that I simply could not doubt their special intention for me that Friday noon hour, and I looked up at the clock to register that it was 12:50 p.m.[2]

Before too long, he was appearing at more and more preaching engagements. Now, however, he preached with a new dimension—a new passion—for he was now happily employed in the Lord's work. Times were tough for him financially, though. He talked about those meager years in a sermon at Bellevue Baptist Church in Memphis, Tennessee, in 1991, at the age of eighty-eight.

> It was a way back in the 1920's when I was a student in Spurgeon's Theological College, London, England. To put it rather bluntly, financially I was broke. I had no income for the mission halls or small churches where I occasionally preached paid no fee. And I would not write home for financial help because at the time my dear sister Margaret was opening, founding a maternity and nursing home and she needed all the financial help she could get.

Well, I was badly in need of a new suit and a new pair of shoes. Those that I had were so worn and shabby I was afraid to preach anywhere in them. After much hesitation I decided that if God would not be too amused I would risk asking Him to send me a new suit.

I was pretty sure that if God bothered to answer at all—this is how He would do it. I would go to preach somewhere and some sympathetic gentleman would say, "Er Brother Baxter, I hope you don't mind my mentioning it but you're needing a new suit and you and I are about the same build, er would you accept one of mine?" And you know, I remember anticipatedly blushing at the very thought of it. But I said well all right God if it has to be that way I agree.

A few days later I received—to my great surprise—I received a letter from a relative whom I had not seen since my babyhood. He was coming on a visit from Australia to England. I can still see the pale blue envelope and paper. In essence, it said this, "Dear Sid. At present, we are sailing through rough winds and choppy waters in the Bay of Biscayne. Somehow, during the past two or three days I have strongly felt to send you the enclosed Bank of England check; perhaps you are needing something. Maybe you could get a new suit."

Well, the check that was enclosed was enough to buy twenty new suits *and* twenty new pairs of shoes. God had fulfilled His word.[3]

On a day-by-day basis Dr. Baxter not only grew in the grace and knowledge of God; he cleaved to, relied on, and trusted him evermore. As a pupil in the Lord's school of instruction, the young preacher Sidlow would learn that the success of his ministry would depend entirely upon the amount of time he spent in prayer with his Master and Savior, the Lord Jesus. He would also learn that God is the rewarder of those who diligently seek him.

His Benefactor

The Bible lists various spiritual gifts: prophecy, teaching, exhortation. But one particular gift is not mentioned: the gift of ministry to teenagers.

In those awkward years of youth, when one is most easily influenced, an older Christian can make a difference in a teenager's life and have lasting effect throughout. This mature Christian who reaches out to the teen seldom realizes his or her import, neither does the teen fully realize the significance of the kindness of the Christian. These rare individuals display an interest in the young person's life. They make an awkward teen feel important—perhaps for the first time. Often, they open their home and treat the teen as one of the family. Their warm beneficence is selfless, caring, considerate, kind. Not only do these spiritual benefactors impart affection, time, and in many cases money; they inspire us to be our best. Quite frequently they succeed in bringing out the best in us. Often our first Bible is one received from their generous hand. They pray for us. They shed tears for us. And often have the privilege of leading us to the Lord.

They genuinely love us with the love of Jesus. For it is Jesus in them that shines forth so radiantly. They help us develop the spiritual disciplines of Bible study, church attendance, and prayer. They are givers without hoping to receive back. They are saints of the Most High, though they seldom realize it. These individuals pass something precious to us like a baton in a relay race. The runner receiving the baton has a responsibility to pass it on to the next runner in the race. They instill in our impressionable hearts a feeling that life does not always operate in the tangible. For when one reflects back over the years, there is a realization that it is the intangible things of life which truly matter. These kindly benefactors are not fully appreciated by the youth at the time of their beneficence. For youth, in its ignorance, seldom appreciates the magnitude and significance of life's treasures at the time they are bestowed. It takes years to pass and stand between the event for a more mature mind to fully comprehend the depth of those experiences—then it is usually too late to say "thank you."

J. Sidlow Baxter had ample opportunity to say "thank you" to his benefactor. He dedicated his magnum opus, *Explore the Book*, to the one who had done so much for him. This man had seen something in Sid. It was obvious to all who knew the teenage Sid that he had likable traits. He carried himself well. He spoke well. He was dependable and trustworthy. He was a hard worker. He was intelligent beyond his years. He was talented and good-looking. But this kindly benefactor saw more than the obvious: He saw a youth who had a hole in his heart, an empty space that the Creator did not occupy. He planted a desire for Bible study in the young man's heart. He was like a father to him—for Sid had a poor excuse of a father. One thing the many-talented Sid lacked was money. He came from a poor family. He took a job as a rent collector to help out his hardworking mother. While Alice would go door-to-door sharing the gospel, Sid would go door-to-door collecting rent. When it came time for him to go to college, there was no money to send him. This is where the largess of the benefactor came in: He paid the tuition all the way through for Sid to attend school in London.

This benefactor was a dear Christian man whose input into one teenager's life made lasting impressions throughout. Inside the covers of *Explore the Book,* the man is named and honored.

41

DEDICATION

These studies are dedicated with deep gratitude and affectionate esteem to my beloved, saintly, and now elderly friend,

JAMES ARTHUR YOXALL, ESQ.,
of Ashton-under-Lyne
and Stalybridge;

my spiritual "father" and gifted teacher in the precious things of Christ; the inspirer of many heavenward aspirings within me, the one who first planted in my youthful heart a zest for Bible study; who has always been to me the ideal Christian gentleman, the choicest of preachers, and, above all, a kindly, experienced older friend ever brimming over with the sanctifying love of the Lord Jesus.[4]

The many men and women whose lives were impacted for eternity through the ministry of Dr. J. Sidlow Baxter say "thank you" as well.

His College

J. Sidlow Baxter would frown if someone commented that he was educated at Spurgeon's College in London. Rather, he would correct them and say he was "trained for the ministry" there. Indeed, trained he was. No other academic institution could have better prepared him for a life of ministry. Charles H. Spurgeon was Sid's hero; and throughout his life he would comment how Spurgeon was the best of the pulpiteers.

The college, founded in 1856, had a list of graduates whose very names could fill a hall of fame. Graham Scroggie (Sid's predecessor to Charlotte Chapel in Edinburgh)

Class of 1924–1928: **Back row from left to right:** H. G. Smith, E. Hassenruck, W. E. Martin, E. Fleischman, F. C. Filewood, C. J. Soar, J. S. Baxter, A. H. Waugh; **Front row from left to right:** A. S. Kerry, W. C. Johnson, R. W. Phillips, E. W. Labrum. J. W. Copeland, W. T. Troll (photos and captions in this chapter courtesy of Spurgeon's College)

was a graduate, as well as W. Y. Fullerton (the author and hymnodist), and Sylvester Whitehorn (who was martyred in China), to name a few.

In 1861, classes moved from a congregational minister's home to the newly built Metropolitan Tabernacle at Newington Butts. Because the Tabernacle lacked accommodations, the college moved again in 1922. A Mr. Charles H. Walker generously donated his house in Falkland Park, and it was here at this mansion (which still functions today as part of the college) that the twenty-two-year-old Sid began his studies.

Spurgeon taught his students to speak plainly and to articulate clearly, and his graduates were the cream of the crop. A deacon once wrote to ask Spurgeon to send him a man who could fill the chapel. Spurgeon replied, "I haven't a man who can fill the chapel but I have several who can fill the pulpit." There was a long history of tradition by the time Sid the student began his training there.

Spurgeon's College football team in 1926. J. Sidlow Baxter, as vice-captain is seated second from the left. An excerpt from the text accompanying this photo reports: "One of the most well-known sons of Spurgeon's College died on the 28th, December 1999 in his 97th year. In a letter written to the College in 1993 in response to a request for information to be included in *The Record*, Sidlow Baxter wrote, 'I am the least of all worthy in the Spurgeon's progeny to merit any such honourable mention'" ("J Sidlow Baxter," *The Record* [June 2000]).

J. Sidlow Baxter loved college. He was always at the "top of his batch" in school. A bright student and a hard worker, he labored long at his class work. It was a thrill for him every morning as he strolled up the stone path that led to the entrance of the college. He knew that had it not been for the magnanimous charity of Mr. Yoxall he would not have had the money to even buy the textbooks for the required classes, much less tuition each year. So as not to be a disappointment to his benefactor, he applied himself all the more.

He was at the Pastors' College from early 1924 to the end of 1928. He was a conscientious student and disciplined Christian; during Lent he would fast on Saturdays, eating only milk and cheese. He loved to read about the giants of the Christian faith, especially the Wesley brothers, John and Charles. He could identify with the Wesley children who owed so much to their godly mother, Susanna. Study-

Pastors' College J. Sidlow Baxter attended from early 1924 to the end of 1928

ing the life of Martin Luther made him contemplate why Luther had such a sense of sinfulness that it overwhelmed him. He was good with languages and did well in Greek. He also enjoyed studying church history.

45

How many college students rewrite portions of their textbooks? Sid did. He took to task one of the authors of one of his church history books. The author was a professor of ecclesiastical history at Yale University. In the margins Sid would carefully write such remarks as, "Rubbish! Wrong! Nothing of the kind! Too weak! How ridiculous is all of this!" He would even go to the extreme of taking a sentence, crossing out a word, and replacing it with one that better fit the idea of the writer or flow of the sentence. On the top page of one of his college notebooks, he wrote, "our will free but feeble!"

Though he relished his time at school, he was lonely for one special person—he missed his sweetheart, Ethel. He wrote her this poem while he was in London in the summer of 1924.

Wembley Reverie

I trod a lonely path, in solitude at night,
No genial lunar face, no silver eye of light
Illumed the dreary folds of interwoven cloud,
The overhanging sky was draped as by a shroud;
When lo, a cloud-rift showed a solitary star,
Which flashed a silvery ray from distance afar!
A momentary gleam, then gone, it shone no more;
And then the darksomeness seemed darker than before.

I loitered mid the trees, one solemn, stilly eve,
No sound broke on the ear, the silence to relieve;
No mournful monody from melancholy breeze,
No trilling melody from songsters in the trees.
When hark, a glorious tune, a shrill, sirenic song
Rang through the arching boughs and avenues along!
The feathered singer soon his sudden song gave o'er;
And then the silence seemed more silent than before.

I loved a lovely flower, a limpid, lovesome thing,
I coveted it much-enamoured, wondering.
It ope'd its petal-face, and blushed a smile one day,
So modest, pure, and shy, it stole my heart away.
I kissed its tender face, I lingered where it grew,
Then left it blooming there: dear Ethel it was you.
And though by many miles we now are far apart,
Love's perfume still enchants my ever-longing heart.
But Providence's hand once gave my flower of flowers
To smile upon me here, for several favoured hours;
My Ethel did indeed from north to south come down,
Her very presence here transfigured London town!
Too soon the visit passed; I saw my flower no more;
And then my lonely heart seemed lonelier than before.[5]

JSB

three

|||||||||||||||||||||||||||||||||||||||||||||||||||||||||||||||||||||||||||||||||||

The Early Marriage

And Adam said, This is now bone of my bones, and flesh of my flesh: she shall be called Woman, because she was taken out of Man.

Genesis 2:23

His Wife Ethel

It is said that doves mate for life. Never apart, they soar the skies of life together until separated by death. Usually, the remaining lovebird is so grief stricken it often dies not long after of a broken heart. Fortunate, but few, are the lovebirds who find true love early while still in youth and have no other loves till death separates.

Sid and Ethel were such lovebirds. Love found them early in youth and sustained them through tribulation and tears, sickness and health. He spoke of her fondly throughout his life, maintaining that there wasn't a time when his heart did not thrill to see "his queen" when she'd enter his study. He speaks of her tenderly in his intimate book, *Divine Healing of the Body*. During the time the manuscript was being edited for publication, she succumbed to cancer and went home to be with the Lord. He writes, "My Ethel and I had been little neighbors when we were only a few years old. We had grown up together. We had gone to the same school. She had never had any sweetheart but me and I none but her. Our union of heart and memory went right back to early childhood."[1]

She was his confidant from his childhood. Ethel typed (sometimes more than once) the manuscripts of twenty volumes that came to publication. She was his travel companion, accompanying him on the many itinerant preaching engagements. And, at the time of her heavenly homecoming, she was about to share in celebrating their golden wedding anniversary. In his book *Does God Still Guide?* he writes of her,

> Forty years ago this year, I became wedded to the dearest, sweetest girl in our town. After the service in the church, we went into the minister's vestry, accompanied by our parents, to sign the marriage register. After the signing, my dear mother gave me a kiss, adding, with a whimsical look, "Well, Sid, my only son, you are now married. You are at the end of all your troubles—this end!" Then she gave us a text from the Bible, which she hoped would be a life-long motto. It was Proverbs 3:5, 6, especially the words, "In all thy ways acknowledge HIM, and He shall direct thy paths."[2]

They were neighbors at five and six years old. They took bicycle rides together. Went to the same school together, had the same friends. Ethel would come visit him in London as he attended Spurgeon's College. In 1927, while still a student in college, Sidlow married his childhood sweet-heart, Ethel Smith. All the years of their lives had been intertwined; from the sunny, love-filled walks as teens over Lancashire's Pennine Hills to the gray, pain-filled days spent in the hospital rooms of Santa Barbara.

Sid, always the romantic, deluged her with poems expressing his love. She made his heart sing. A poem he wrote her when they were still young reflects his heart's desire. It was written July 2, 1923, four years before they married. It is an acrostic, and careful inspection reveals her name and address: Ethel Smith, Twenty Melville Street.

A Sunset Acrostic

Evening whispers "Day is done",
Tranquil sinks the westering sun,
Heaven's ablush with crimson light
E'er he kisses earth "Good night";
Lovely, lonely even.

Softly sighs the soothing breeze,
Moving mid the murmuring trees,
Idle thrushes seek the nest,
Toilsome day dies in the west;
Hush, tired earth, 'tis night.

Twenty topaz-tints all shewing
Make the sunset's final glowing
Exquisite beyond the knowing;
Lovely hues and colours growing
Velvet flames on earth are throwing,
Intimating day is going;
Lapping lake and streamlet flowing,
Languid breeze, so softly blowing,
Eve, how sweet thy spell!
Sunset's tulip-tinted view

On January 30, 1927, at age 24, while still a student in college, Sidlow married his childhood sweetheart, Ethel Smith. The ceremony was held at Stamford St. Methodist Church.

Tires too soon and bids adieu,
Rapidly each lovely hue
Ebbs more quickly than it grew,
Ever deepening shades pursue—
Trim the lamps, 'tis night.[3]

JSB

His Long Companion

The Baxters were a couple "on the go." Once Sidlow became more widely known in Canada and the United States, he and Ethel traveled all the time. Not only did they cover the forty-eight states of the North American continent, their nonstop tour took them to such exotic places as India, Egypt, Palestine, Africa, and the Caribbean. Eight times they visited the United States and Canada. Wherever he went she was with him.

Speaking engagements kept pouring in and his faithful wife was ever ready to accompany him. Ethel helped in the planning of the meetings; she helped him pray regarding the selection of the bookings. She was his prayer partner as well as his helpmeet.

From childhood to golden wedding anniversary, Ethel was his long companion and colaborer in the faith. In Edinburgh she conducted Bible studies for the ladies of the church. She helped prepare his manuscripts for publication. She was selfless in her love for him. When she learned she had cancer,

Sid and Ethel visiting their nephew Cliff and family in Staten Island, New York, 1955

she did not tell him until they had completed a speaking tour of the Greek Islands because she did not want to interfere with his preaching.

Reminiscing about her as a young child of eight, he describes her in his novel (now out of print) *The Hidden Hand*. "To say the least, she was a super-normally beautiful child. It was not only the light, wavy hair, the pink complexion, the soft yet beaming blue eyes, and the finely chiseled features; there was something about that face which exceeded unusual prettiness. It was so strikingly pure; almost as though some young, heavenly cherub was shining through it."[4]

She was not only the delight of his heart, she was also a devoted Christian, sensitive to the things of God.

> One Sunday morning, just as my dear wife was entering her usual pew at church, she became strangely but irresistibly constrained to change place and sit near the front, with a certain lady who at the time was beset by sore trial. Momentarily she hesitated lest her unusual action should give a wrong impression to those around, or cause embarrassment to the

Sid and Ethel sometime during the 1970s

lady herself. Yet along with the surprise urge came a peaceful assurance that it was of the Spirit; so she acted accordingly. It was not until eight or nine months later that she learned what this bit of obeyed guidance had meant. The saintly woman with whom my dear wife went to sit had been struggling with the problem as to whether she should still come to church, owing to the ugly scandal now associated with the family

54

name. She was scared of curious looks and questions. She had pleaded, "Dear Lord, guide me. Preserve me from unwise enquirers; and, if it please Thee, give me a sign: may Mrs. Baxter be led to come and sit with me." This, by the way, is an instance in which guidance prayed for by one person was answered through guidance given to another.[5]

Together they shared life's riches of joy and its disappointments of sorrow. In 1977 God called Ethel home to heaven, leaving the bereaved widower to roam his little house wishing he could hear her footsteps once more.

His Dear Daughter

During the pastorate at Northampton, England, Ethel gave birth to their only child, a daughter. Miriam Ethel Baxter was born on November 16, 1929. How they adored that bonny lassie! His tenderness toward her is seen in a story about her in *Majesty, The God You Should Know.*

When my dear daughter was just a chubby, dimple-faced little girl, her uncle Sam made her a birthday present of a charming little wicker chair. Besides its pretty appearance, it had the auricular novelty that when sat upon it played a merry tune. It quickly became a great favorite. Our little Miriam would sit and stand, and sit and stand, and as she did so the music started and stopped, and started and stopped. It gave so much pleasure (I do not mind telling you secretly that sometimes, when mommie and Mim were not around, daddy used to sit on that little chair. The one problem was that when he got up, the chair got up too!). But what I want to tell you is this: Again and again when our little one sat on that chair and the pleasant music started, an inner voice would whisper to me, "Sid, Sid, the promises of God are like that chair—they only play their music to those who rest in them!"[6]

When the Baxters moved to Scotland for Sid to take the pastorate at Charlotte Chapel in Edinburgh, Miriam was just eight years old. She was a pleasant, pretty girl and shared in her daddy's love for music. As she grew up she wanted to be a music teacher. But the world came in and shut the Lord out. She drifted from the church as she grew. Finally, she disappeared from the landscape, and it broke Sid's and Ethel's hearts. The tears of a parent over a child lost to the world can never be healed this side of heaven.

The love he had for her, and his concern for her welfare, is expressed in a little poem written to her when she lay sick with the mumps. Here is the poem he wrote to his dear bonny lassie:

Sympathetic Lines of a Father to a Daughter in Bed with Mumps

When Nature's laws young folk abuse,
How sternly she exacts her dues!
When pleasure-mad they lose their sleep,
Whole days in bed she makes them keep!
Then, if they still rebel—the chumps,
She sends neuralgia, or the mumps;
And if they will not learn from these,
She sends some really fell disease;
And if they still her rule defy,
There's nothing for it—they must die.
If only children could admit
That parents know a tiny bit . . .
But what a nuisance parents are!
Why, modern youth is wiser far!
Our parents never had such schools!
What! Do they think young folk are fools?
We'll show them whether we have sense,
And teach them it is THEY who're dense!

There's one thing nowadays quite clear—
That parents should not interfere.

Thus generations come and go;
From youth to age they wiser grow;
Yet as they pass they all relate
They learn life's lessons—just too late.
Our junior wisecracks dodge the truth
That dense old parents once were youth,
That they themselves must older grow,
Oft haunted by, "I told you so",
And all their youthful bombast rue
When they as parents suffer too!

When they as parents suffer too,
As with strange certainty they do,
THEY marvel at the blooming cheek
The NEXT relay of youth can speak;
They hear the same old arguments
Arrayed in fresh accoutrements—
The times are different, so are we,
Just let us have our way, and see.
For artful Nature oft repays
Her rebels in ironic ways.

Thus generations, as they go,
Perpetuate the tale of woe.
They will not learn from yesterday,
But choose to learn the harder way—
"Experience" shall be teacher, please;
And well he teaches—but what fees!
What fees he charges those he schools,
Before he makes wise men of fools!
How oft flogged scholars have confessed,
"Ah yes, poor Dad and Mum knew best!"
How many in that same hard school
Have learned relentless Nature's rule!

And praised the parents once they blamed,
And deeply humbled have exclaimed,
"If only I had understood,
How truly they advised for good!
And now my own short youth is fled,
And both my parents now are dead;
Oh, why will not MY children heed,
When now with wise mind I plead?"

Each generation soon is past,
So sure at first, so sad at last.
As ranks of youth successive rise,
Each thinks, "We are supremely wise".
Each rank of youth more knowledge knows,
Yet each a bit less wisdom shows;
Wisdom is knowledge rightly used;
Knowledge is folly when abused.
New youth new knowledge ever learns,
But wisdom's USE of knowledge spurns.

Old fashioned parents, hold your tongue!
How dare you think your children wrong?
How dare you scold, advise, command?
You simply do not understand!
Remember you have HAD your day!
And WE prefer to learn OUR way!
And so we might go on and on,
Till generations all were gone;
But wisdom says it now is time
To terminate this mournful rhyme.

If these few lines should e'er forsooth
Confront the eyes of some proud youth,
Then may they have the good effect
Of making such a one reflect—
Mere knowledge does not make one wise,
Let those who would true wisdom gain

Their parent's counsels not disdain.
Remember this, all else above,

THEIR counsel ever springs from LOVE.
If their response at times seems slow,
Perhaps they know things YOU DON'T know;
And if in BRAIN they lag behind,
They have at least a wiser MIND!
And all within yourself, of worth,
They gave you, when they gave you birth.
That wise old Fifth Command revere—
Honour your parents while they're here;
And you will find in later days
What handsome dividends it pays.

AUTHOR UNKNOWN BECAUSE
OF EXTREME MODESTY[7]

Sometimes the wandering sheep returns to the fold—and sometimes it does not. Sid never gave up praying for Miriam to return to the Lord, though at times he felt the heavens were as brass and God had deaf ears. Still, he maintained his vigil of prayer for her throughout his life.

In 1977 he composed a birthday greeting for her. In it he still faithfully points the way to God:

Oh, for some word of wit and weight
Now Miriam is forty-eight!
Ye Muses, whisper in mine ear
Some secret word of birthday cheer:
The years fly by; what can we say?
Like fugitives they steal away!
Just ponder it, and get it straight:
Our little "Mim" now forty-eight!
It seems to us but yesterday—
That bonnie girlie bright and gay—
Those jolly days of skates and bikes,

Sidlow, Miriam, and Ethel in Northampton, England

Of Edinburgh and Ravelston Dykes!
Those glamor years! One wonders how
They fled so soon: where are they now?
How shall their story now be told?
For this poor penman is too old:
And so, despite the wish to write
Some birthday poem sparkling bright,
I'll simply say; God bless you, Mim,
And let you know you're dear to Him,
And fill the days with precious freight
Especially now you're forty-eight:
And as the "Muse" within us burns
We'll wish you "MANY HAPPY RETURNS".[8]

J. Sidlow Baxter was estranged from his daughter, Miriam;
for the last twenty years of his life he never saw her. They
exchanged birthday cards each year and talked on the phone

occasionally. The last four years of his life he lost complete contact with her. He even hired a private investigator to try and locate her—but to no avail. Sid assumed she had passed away somewhere. She was not at his funeral. To this day she remains an enigma.

After his death this poem was found in his personal belongings.

Missing

Each little toy you loved so much
Is begging for your baby touch;
    In every nook and corner you are missing;
Your cradle in the nursery,
Your mother's arms your daddy's knee,
    In every nook and corner you are missing.
        Your little soldiers
        Are lying on the shelf so blue;
        They march no more across the floor,
        They miss their captain true.
The dawn still finds the morning sun,
But in this heart, my little one,
In every nook and corner you are missing.[9]

JSB

four

|||||||||||||||||||||||||||||||||||||||||||||||||||||||||||||||||||||||||||||||||||

THE EARLY PASTORATES

> Neglect not the gift that is in thee, which was given thee by prophecy, with the laying on of the hands of the presbytery.
>
> 1 TIMOTHY 4:14

His First: Northampton

In 1929 J. Sidlow Baxter accepted his first pastorate. With seminary behind him, and God's calling upon him, the twenty-six-year-old was ready to take on the responsibilities of a pastor. He had several invitations to thriving churches but, after much prayer, turned each of them down. He felt led to go to a "ne'er do well" (his own description) church in the English midlands. The church was quite small and in desperate need of someone to come in and try to grow the declining congregation.

He accepted the challenge, viewing it as an opportunity to further hone his preaching skills while at the same time be obedient to the Lord. His dear Ethel was busy keeping the house and being mother to their darling baby Miriam, who was born in November of that year. Much of the young pastor's time was spent getting to know the elders and deacons and church body. He had a vision for the little church and the surrounding community. He began having congregational prayer meetings that grew into cottage prayer meetings, each uniting with one purpose—revival.

The demands of growing a small church and raising a family kept him busy. However, he still took time to visit the countryside and commune with nature. One of his favorite things to do in Northampton was to visit the village of Moulton. Moulton was famous for producing the "Father of Modern Missions," William Carey. Sid enjoyed visiting the little Carey cottage and seeing the trough where Carey the cobbler had soaked his leather. It made him think of world missions—later in life he would be a big supporter of foreign mission work.

The long hours spent on his knees and in church behind the pulpit began to pay off. The little congregation was growing. The Holy Spirit blessed it with revival, something which would occur in each of his three pastorates. The young pastor met with the elders to discuss building onto the existing premises to accommodate more parishioners. There would be a big cost to have the building suitably adapted. A generous offer came in to build a new church in a better area, which would solve all their problems, but the members said, "No." J. Sidlow Baxter began at once to seek God's guidance to a different pastorate altogether. His two-year training ground was drawing to a close. God would not keep his servant stagnant.

His Second: Sunderland

A call to pastor a church came from northeast England in 1931. Sidlow, Ethel, and little Miriam would eventually pack their little belongings and move to Sunderland to accept the pastorate at Bethesda Church. But the decision was not an easy one, either for Sid or the deacons of Bethesda Church.

There is a story about C. H. Spurgeon that best illustrates Baxter's success as a preacher. The first student of Spurgeon's College once came into Spurgeon's office complaining that he had been preaching for three months without one soul being converted. "Why," said Spurgeon, "you don't expect conversions every time you open your mouth, do you?" "Of course not," was the answer. "Then that is the reason you haven't had them," he replied.

Every time Sid opened his mouth to preach, he fully expected heaven to come down and the Holy Spirit to do his work. Word was getting out that a very remarkable preacher by the name of J. Sidlow Baxter was causing stirs here and there. He relates the interesting story of how he came to Bethesda Church in *Does God Still Guide?* Speaking of himself, he writes,

> Inward conviction and outward direction blended as he now sought guidance about a new sphere. Five invitations came, one after another, to churches in London. He visited each in turn; yet although each gave a unanimous "call", the inner voice said "No".
>
> Months passed; then came an invitation from away up northeast. Rather reluctantly he went, saying, "Who wants to live there, the edge o' beyond?" Yet as he entered the pulpit on the Sunday morning, two impressions at once registered: (1) "What a drab place!" (2) "This is where you

are coming." The Elders met after the service; they knew, too, just as definitely. Guidance was unmistakable.

Is that all? No. That influential church had been without a pastor two years. The office bearers were cautious, and had decided that on no account should that large church have a young pastor. Yet strangely enough, three letters had come simultaneously, all recommending this same "young man". The first of these letters was from an outstanding minister whose urge to write had come suddenly one morning while he was shaving. The second was from a well-known Christian leader who had wakened during the night with a curious impression that he must write. The third was from a college principal who had written under similar constraint. It looked like guidance; but the minister whom they all named was a young man; so he was put right at the end of the "candidates" list, and only invited even then as a courtesy to the three writers. Eventually an older minister from up north was at the point of being chosen. He was to preach for them once again with the almost foregone conclusion that he was "the man". The Sunday prior to that, the undesired young minister came. He was younger than any of their former ministers; yet at once he knew, and they knew, and all knew, that he was to be their next pastor. From the beginning there was blessing; and during the third year supernatural revival visited that church with very blessed effects in many hearts, and such incoming crowds that there had to be two evening services each Sunday.

Was even that all? No; God had overruled the ten months or so during which those well-meaning Elders had pushed the young minister's name to the end of their list. It was during those months that his five preachings in London took place. Later, when special commitments took him to London, he found the way wonderfully prepared through contacts made on those five visits![1]

C. H. Spurgeon was known to have said the following in regard to pastors selecting a church: "A large church is to be preferred to a small one. The latter has many attractions, but it is not unlike a rowboat which a man is in danger of upsetting if he moves about, whereas the former is like an ocean steamer, on which he can parade without the possibility of upsetting the whole concern."[2]

J. Sidlow Baxter took on the large church in Sunderland with its twelve elders and twenty-six deacons with nervous excitement, for he was full of inexperience. Bethesda Church had a rich history as a Bible church and its previous pastor, W. Graham Scroggie, had left a large footprint for the young Sid to fill. Yet it wasn't long before he was welcomed and the members took to him like bees to honey. And there was a buzz about him amongst Christians in the surrounding regions. Soon the young pastor's reputation for articulate pulpit mastery and heaven-sent revival was spreading like a swarm of bees all the way to the bonny banks of Scotland.

five

THE EDINBURGH PASTORATE

For a bishop must be blameless, as the steward of God; not selfwilled, not soon angry, not given to wine, no striker, not given to filthy lucre; but a lover of hospitality, a lover of good men, sober, just, holy, temperate; holding fast the faithful word as he hath been taught, that he may be able by sound doctrine both to exhort and to convince the gainsayers.

TITUS 1:7–9

His Predecessor

The elders of Charlotte Chapel in Edinburgh had been hoping for some time that J. Sidlow Baxter would accept their invitation to become their pastor. It was 1935 and things were changing both in the landscape of their city and across the globe. One could hear first echoes of the

J. Sidlow Baxter, Northampton, England

jingoistic marching boots of Hitler's army as they began to stomp forth from Nazi Germany, ultimately reaching a declaration of war in 1939. Also, ever since the Scottish Enlightenment of the eighteenth century, Edinburgh had become the intellectual hotbed of Western Europe. Pulpits were occupied by scholars who brought forth deep sermons in an attempt to reach smart congregations, often comprised of scientists and men of learning.

There had been other "evils" in addition to the horror of Hitler's armies. J. Sidlow Baxter wrote of these in the *Charlotte Chapel Record*, while pastor there in February of 1944.

But long before Hitler assaulted Europe with his Nazi hordes in 1939, Germany had launched a very different sort of war on Europe; and in this earlier war the weapons were not planes and bombs and tanks and guns, but pens and books and classroom desks and pulpits and magazine articles. This was the war of the German "Higher Criticism" against the citadels of evangelical Christianity. There is nothing wrong with the so-called "Higher Criticism" in itself, considered simply as one branch of Biblical research and scholarship, occupied with the historic origins and human authorships of the books in our Bible: but the rationalistic German brand of the "Higher Criticism" to which I now refer was nothing other than a propagandism designed to degrade the Bible to the level of a merely human book. All the erudition and patient subtlety for which German scholarship had become justly famed were prostituted without reserve to encompass this ignoble objective.

Like a huge octopus, the movement spread its ugly arms out over Germany and Holland and France and Britain and America.[1]

Charlotte Baptist Chapel in Edinburgh, Scotland

Charlotte Baptist Chapel on West Rose Street in Edinburgh had its pulpit protected from liberalism with the preaching of their very famous pastor, W. Graham Scroggie. Born in 1877 in Great Malvern, England, William Graham Scroggie was a giant in the faith. His reputation as a pulpit master was fostered by his scholarly and practical exposition of the Bible; his fame grew immediately after graduating from Spurgeon's Pastors' College in London. An opponent of liberalism, he was forced to leave his first two ministries due to his conservative stand on the Bible. Widely known for being a scholar, Scroggie had a doctor of divinity degree conferred upon him in 1927 by the University of Edinburgh. He was a master at Biblical exposition. In his commentary on the twenty-third Psalm, his talents are readily apparent:

The Shepherd is none other than the Lord Himself, and the sheep is none other than I. Of course, there is a flock, but it is not in view just now; only my Lord and I. This relationship is intensely individual, and no element of selfishness need obtrude as each of us thinks of himself and his Lord. With me were poverty and emptiness, but with Him, riches and abundance. My poverty once made Him poor, but now His riches make me rich; never again need I want. I was often weary, but He is always strong. Once my weariness made Him weary, but now His strength makes me strong. I knew only the rough and noisy places, but He knows the places soft and quiet. Once He came into the rough and noise for me, and now I dwell in the pastures of tender grass, and beside the waters of quietness with Him.[2]

When Scroggie left the pulpit of Charlotte Chapel to pursue an itinerant ministry that would take him all over the world, the elders had to replace him with a man with similar attributes—one who was scholarly, practical, and who stood against the growing liberalism of the day. They could come up with only one candidate who fit the bill: J. Sidlow Baxter.

His Church

During the time of the Second World War, British Christians often said that "The South was covered by the preaching of D. Martyn Lloyd-Jones and the North was covered by J. Sidlow Baxter." Both Baxter and Lloyd-Jones took the pastorates of churches that were steeped in a rich history of previous pulpit greatness. The great G. Campbell Morgan had thrilled audiences at Westminster Chapel in London—Lloyd-Jones took the pulpit at Westminster Chapel and filled it aptly. W. Graham Scroggie expounded truth

71

from the pulpit at Charlotte Chapel in Edinburgh—and J. Sidlow Baxter filled it aptly.

The rich history of Charlotte Baptist Chapel began in 1808 when a young Christian businessman named Christopher Anderson decided to begin outreach works in one of the suburbs of his native city of Edinburgh. God blessed the work and in 1818 the church moved to Rose Street at the west end of Edinburgh. The edifice remains to this day.

So it was here at Charlotte Chapel in Edinburgh where J. Sidlow Baxter preached for eighteen years, and his anointed ministry touched thousands of hearts in the capital city of Scotland. The Lord's hand upon Sidlow's pastorate began to show itself immediately: at the first evening service he preached, six people were saved. The word got out quickly around town about the young man who was preaching to overflowing crowds at both services on Sunday.

The church seated one thousand, which was large for its day, and it wasn't long before the office-bearers agreed to put speakers in the basement to accommodate the swelling congregation, who could not all fit inside the chapel. Sid fell in love with his church, and his selfless attitude towards it was reflected by his action of taking his salary and putting it entirely back into the church. He never bought a home in Edinburgh, nor did he ever purchase an automobile. He walked to church each day from a long distance, even in bad weather, to save the expense of a car. And through that humble servant of the Lord, many there were led to the mission field and ministry service.

The outstanding feature of Dr. Baxter's ministry in Edinburgh was his Thursday evening Bible school, which comprises the body of *Explore the Book*, his remarkable commentary on the entire Bible. These Thursday evening Bible lectures in the Chapel are still talked about in Edinburgh today. "The Course," he said, "was meant to give a practical grip on the Bible as a whole." He describes the method of study as "interpretive"; his aim was "to get hold of the controlling thought, the outstanding meaning and message of each book and then see it in relation to the other books of the Scriptures."[3]

> The Second World War (1939 to 1945) brought many problems. Young men and women were called up for service in the armed forces and it was not easy to replace the vacancies in the various organisations. For a "Down Town Church" such as Charlotte Chapel, the black-out created peculiar difficulties. Not only was it difficult to black-out the main Church building, together with its halls and rooms, but many members, especially the elderly, found it impossible to be present at the Sunday evening services and the week-night meetings. This presented a challenge and Mr. Baxter met it by arranging an afternoon service in addition to the two other services, every Sunday. He put every ounce of energy into this heavy programme and carried it through successfully. As the war continued conditions became more stringent. Many of the older men were called up for service in the Home Guard and were on duty most Sundays. Other war-time organisations demanded their quotas of both men and women. It meant six years of unparalleled difficulties and frustrations. When the war broke out the membership had reached it highest total ever of 1,129. *The Record* had reached its highest circulation as also had the tract distribution. Mr. Baxter wrote the tract *The Lightbringer* and 10,000 were being distributed monthly. The war dealt a heavy blow at this work. One cannot pay too great a tribute to Mr. Baxter for his dedicated leadership during those difficult war years.[4]

The church of Charlotte Baptist Chapel, though rich in history, is like any other church: its physical building does not determine success but the people who comprise the church—their dedication to service and prayer ultimately decides the direction of church progress.

His Congregation

The members of Charlotte Baptist Chapel in Edinburgh were accustomed to good preaching. They recognized clearly when greatness emanated from the half-moon pulpit, so when J. Sidlow Baxter was first offered the pastorate there, he hesitated: "I was waiting for the ghost of Graham Scroggie to get out."[5] He was unsure of himself in scholarly Edinburgh. Eventually though, the thirty-two-year-old Sid acquiesced and, as usual, when he felt God leading he obediently followed, so off were the Baxters to answer the call to Edinburgh. Though full of misgivings initially, he soon settled into the new environment and quickly fell in love with the people there. They warmly accepted him and a mutual bond of love was established from the very beginning of his long eighteen-year pastorate there. It would be a time of prophetic preaching for him as well as a prolific time of written ministry.

Scotland has a magical history beset with bloody wars and valiant clansmen. Many a foe had been laid low with the brandished Claymore—the Claymore sword was a fifteenth century two-handed, Scottish sword that had a cross-guard "v" shape which was designed to block sword cuts and disarm the enemy at the same time. In the same manner, the prophetic preaching of Baxter laid his congregation low in bowed abeyance to a holy God. He talked openly about the spiritual visitation he experienced in the pulpit there in a sermon he preached at Bellevue Baptist Church in 1977.

> Edinburgh you know has a psychology all its own. It's a collegiate city—a university city. And it's the Athens of the

Charlotte Baptist Chapel
OFFICE-BEARERS 1953

Top left: J. Begg; Top right: J. McGuinness; Back row from left to right: J. Cochrane, J. Balmer, D. L. Macnair, J. Cossar, J. Oliphant; Third row from left to right: J. Whitlie, D. M. Jenkins, J. Ritchie, D. S. Cormack, D. Blair, J. Hudson, J. E. Coutts, D. S. Steele; Second row from left to right: D. Petrie, J. B. Purves, T. Currie, W. A. D. Somerville, W. C. Tullis, J. M. Tullis, G. Davidson, R. Hadden, D. M. Murray, G. H. Rae, G. Rae; First row from left to right: J. Bethune, P. Armstrong, R. D. Clark, W. M. Urquhart, Rev. J. Sidlow Baxter, R. Aitken, R. J. Gillon, P. B. Murray, J. Paterson

British Isles where all the wiseacres gather and stroke their intellectual beards. And I went there when I was only 32 and I looked very young and I had a mass of golden hair at that time, alas lamentations how is the gold become dim. However, that was that. And I had many misgivings—they had such scholars in the pulpits in Edinburgh. I thought, "Sid how on earth will you make out here?" But you know in the third year we had a visitation from heaven. The whole church was gripped with revival. Do you know how it began? I'll tell you. One Sunday morning when I came out of my vestry and went up the semi-circular stairway to the half-moon shaped pulpit; just as I got to the top stair, ooh there was no mistaking it, it was just as though I had entered some invisible envelopment. However, I couldn't

75

pause on the top step I had to go forward which I did. I went to the pulpit desk and bowed in prayer as we always do there. And just behind me, in the alcove, the choir sang the usual little devotional introit and then I just lifted up my hands and the whole church was down in prayer. And all through the service I was conscious of a most wonderful felicity of utterance. Whether they noticed it or not I don't know. But I felt it. Anyway, I would have dismissed it from mind only when I came out of the vestry the next Sunday, the same thing happened at the same moment on the same top stair. Hmm. Well again I would have dismissed it from mind but it happened again the next Sunday. Now are you beginning to think that I'm the imaginable type? Well you're wrong. I'm the opposite. There's not one article of my faith that I haven't had to fight for intellectually. I'm rather the other way. And I'm still rather dubious about people who have too many visions. But I had now to mention it to Ethel—which I did. You know, it was from then that big things started to happen. I didn't learn until eight months later that a retired head mistress of a girl's college (Miss Janet Rogerson) had made a compact with eight or nine other women; that every day they would pray for their young, golden-haired new pastor. And that once a week they would meet together to pray for him, coordinating it in that way. And do you know what the covenant was? They prayed every day and then together once a week that every time the young minister went into the pulpit, he would become consciously clothed with the Holy Spirit.[6]

Actually, the revival at Charlotte Chapel was so intense, and God's Spirit so real, that when Baxter stepped into the pulpit to begin to pray, the congregation began to weep. After the service was ended and Baxter had left the sanctuary, people remained motionless and silent in prayer. Many new converts were added to God's kingdom during this time, and Baxter gave the glory to God.

CHARLOTTE CHAPEL RECORD.

Charlotte Baptist Chapel, W. Rose Street, Edinburgh.

Editor · · · · ·	*Rev. J. Sidlow Baxter*
Assist. Editor · · · ·	*Miss E. Boyle*
"*Record*" *Secretary* · · ·	*Mr J. E. Coutts*

VOL. 38—No. 2   **FEBRUARY 1944.**   PRICE THREEPENCE

The Bible and the War.

By the Rev. J. SIDLOW BAXTER.

The Bible and the war—no subject could be more relevant than this to-day; and no subject could be more important. The Bible and the present war have a close connection with each other. Few people may realise this; but it is certainly true. Few people may bother their heads about it; but if the people of Britain and Europe hath bothered their heads a bit more about the Bible in the pre-war days, the present madness of bloodshed might have been averted. I wish to speak here about the Bible and the war in a threefold way—first, the Bible and the *pre*-war period; then the Bible and the *mid*-war period; then the Bible and the *post*-war period.

First, then, think about the Bible and the *pre*-war period. Shall we ever forget that day in September 1939, when the fateful news came to us over the radio that once again Britain was at war with Germany? And What a war it is which that evil day brought upon us! Little did most of us realise at that time the full extent of Germany's preparedness. Little did most of us realise the extremity of Britain's *un*preparedness. Germany had carefully planned for years in advance. Hitler's " Fifth Columnists " had infiltrated into every part of Europe, and were ready to do their dirty work to the tick of the clock.

But long before Hitler assaulted Europe with his Nazi hordes in 1939, Germany had launched a very different sort of war on Europe; and in this earlier war the weapons were not planes and bombs and tanks and guns, but pens and books and class-room desks and pulpits and magazine articles. This was the war of the German " Higher Criticism " against the citadels of evangelical Christianity. There is nothing wrong with the so-called " Higher Criticism " in itself, considered simply as one branch of Biblical research and scholarship, occupied with the historic origins and human authorships of the books in our Bible : but the rationalistic German brand of the " Higher Criticism " to which I now refer was nothing other than a propagandism designed to degrade the Bible to the level of a merely human book. All the erudition and patient subtlety for which German scholarship had become justly famed were prostituted without reserve to encompass this ignoble objective.

Like a huge octopus, the movement spread its ugly arms out over Germany and Holland and France and Britain and America, through the pens of Eichorn and Schleirmacher and Palus and De Wette and Vatke and Kuenen and Wellhausen and others. Like a theological Nazism, it distributed its " Fifth Columnists " in the pulpits and schools of all the Protestant denominations on the Continent, and then secured " Quislings " in Britain and America, in the persons of such leaders as doctors Samuel Davidson, Robertson Smith, S. R. Driver, C. A. Briggs, and the recently-

His Sermons

There are "seasons" in a person's life which surmount the ordinary. They stand out like bright gold against dull granite. At times, athletes have these moments, resulting in a new baseball home run record or a golf grand slam. Then time erodes the luster of the individual's natural ability, though the record of achievement remains for perpetuity. The Christian life is like that of the athlete. There is discipline involved as well as concentration. Also there is a hope of victory and at times defeat. The book of Hebrews states, "let us run with patience the race that is set before us" (Heb. 12:1). And Paul stated, while awaiting certain death in a dank Roman prison, "I have fought a good fight, I have finished my course, I have kept the faith" (2 Tim. 4:7). When J. Sidlow Baxter was pastor of Charlotte Chapel in Edinburgh during the nervous years of the Second World War, he simply was in his "prime." If one should doubt that statement, obtain a copy of his *Explore the Book*, which is comprised of his Thursday evening meetings at that hallowed church. It was there in the capital of Scotland that his preaching took on prophetic tones and bowed a congregation in humility before an almighty God.

The following is a sample of his preaching during that momentous time. Previously published in his little gem of a book, *Does God Still Guide?*, it is a good representation of his style as a preacher. Here it is in its entirety, including a short introduction by Baxter:

> My mind goes back to a sermon which I preached on this theme, years ago, in Edinburgh, Scotland. Its title was: THE DELAYS OF JESUS, and its introductory text was John 6:17, "It was now dark, and Jesus was not come to them." That sermon was preached just as the Second World War was ending with the collapse of Nazi Germany and the

suicide of Adolf Hitler. Sitting in our church on a Sunday morning was a padre who at that time was over in Britain with the American forces. Now that the war was over, at least in its European theatre, his heart had been thrilling at the thought of his soon being returned to America, to his precious wife, and to his dear little son whom he had not yet even seen, owing to prolonged war-time absence. Then, like a sudden, stunning blow, word had come that he was assigned to immediate new duty in Japan for an indefinite period. His despondency as he sat in our Sunday morning service, with that on his mind, need not be described. Earnest prayer, mounting hope, and now this sudden, sickening delay! I did not know him, had never met him, and knew nothing of his sadness, but I had at least one unusually attentive hearer that morning when I announced as my subject: the problem of divinely permitted delays!

And now, just recently, I have been privileged to hold meetings at a large church in Texas. Its beloved pastor is one of the most gifted, consecrated ministers whom I have ever had the pleasure to serve. I did not know him until then, and was surprised when he told me that he had met me and heard me preach twenty years earlier. He took from a locked drawer his carefully treasured war diary, and read to me his record of that Sunday morning service in Edinburgh, Scotland, twenty years earlier, and how God had spoken to him through that discourse on divine delays!

That sermon has never been printed, taped, or even preached again from then until now; but I have a feeling that it should have a resurrection in these pages. Whether it seems the propitious thing to reintroduce it here, practically as it was given then, I will not stay to determine; but it seems to speak the very word which I am wanting to say here on this problem of divine delays. So, here it is.

THE DELAYS OF JESUS

"It was now dark, and Jesus was not come to them."

—JOHN 6:17

79

These words take our thoughts back to a dark and stormy night on the Sea of Galilee long ago. A small vessel lurched and lunged and creaked and groaned amid the swirling waves of a heavy storm. A point had come when oars seemed useless, and hope was almost gone. One thought alone—one anxious, puzzled, almost despairing thought—betrayed itself through the strained looks of those twelve men on board: Why had the Master not come? Had they not rightly understood Him to mean that He would be with them long ere this? Yet, "it was now dark and Jesus was not come to them". Why, why the delay?

Such is the immediate connection of the text. But look at the words again: "It was now dark and Jesus was not come to them." Do the words suggest anything beyond their immediate connection? I think they do. They somehow open a theme which, although it may seem strange at first, is of very tender concern to all Christian hearts. I mean the delays of Jesus.

All of us who have had any mentionable experience of the Christian life have had times when we, too, have been perplexed by the delays, or seeming delays, of our heavenly Master. He has sometimes kept us waiting (though with gracious purpose which we did not know at the time) until we were at the point of soul-agony, and we groaned, like those long-ago disciples, "It is now dark, and Jesus has not come."

In the Gospel records there are three noteworthy instances of such delay by our Lord Jesus, and we may learn much from them for our guidance and comfort. Let me call your attention to them again, just here. First, there is the delay with which our text is connected, namely, our Lord's delay in going to the disciples on the night of that severe storm. Second, there was His seemingly unsympathetic delay while on the way to heal the daughter of Jairus. Third, there was His strange delay before going to Bethany after receiving word from Martha and Mary, "Lord, behold, he whom Thou lovest is sick."

Yes, I think we may learn much from these delays of Jesus; and it will help us if we consider them in a threefold way: (1) their outward strangeness, (2) their inward purpose, (3) their lasting message.

THEIR OUTWARD STRANGENESS

So, then, to begin with, we notice their outward strangeness. How strange indeed seemed our Lord's delay in relieving those disciples amid that pounding night-storm on Galilee! The incident is recorded by Matthew and Mark and John. They make quite clear that the storm was a bad one; but the most striking evidence of its fury and the plight of the disciples is supplied by John's remark that when at last Jesus walked to them over the turmoiled waters, they had rowed only "five and twenty or thirty furlongs" (three miles or so) even though it was now "the fourth watch of the night" (Matt. 14:25). Formerly the Jews had divided the night into three watches, but after Palestine became a Roman province the Roman division into four was adopted. The first watch ran from 6 p.m. till 9; the second from 9 till midnight; the third from 12 o'clock midnight till 3 a.m., and the "fourth watch of the night" was from 3 a.m. till 6 a.m., at which point daytime reckoning began again. So, then, if our Lord came to them in "the fourth watch", they had been struggling with the oars from evening onward (John 6:16) for over nine or ten hours—and, after all that, they had covered only three miles or so! To all appearances they were in acute peril, yet Jesus made no move to go to them until that darkest hour just before the dawn; and His delay is made all the stranger by Mark's comment that from the mountain elevation where our Lord prayed, "He saw them toiling in rowing".

But now we leave that storm for a very different scene. In Mark 5:22–36 we see our Lord's delay while on His way to heal the daughter of Jairus. The account reads:

81

"And, behold, there cometh one of the rulers of the synagogue, Jairus by name; and when he saw Jesus, he fell at His feet, and besought Him greatly, saying, My little daughter lieth at the point of death: I pray thee, come and lay thy hands on her, that she may be healed; and she shall live. And Jesus went with him; and much people followed him, and thronged him. And a certain woman, which had an issue of blood twelve years, and had suffered many things of many physicians, and had spent all that she had, and was nothing bettered, but rather grew worse, when she had heard of Jesus, came in the press behind, and touched his garment. For she said, If I may touch but his clothes, I shall be whole. And straightway the fountain of her blood was dried up; and she felt in her body that she was healed of that plague. And Jesus, immediately knowing in himself that virtue had gone out of him, turned him about in the press, and said, Who touched my clothes? His disciples said unto him, Thou seest the multitude thronging thee, and sayest thou, Who touched me? And he looked round about to see her that had done this thing. But the woman fearing and trembling, knowing what was done in her, came and fell down before him, and told him all the truth. And he said unto her, Daughter, thy faith hath made thee whole; go in peace, and be whole of thy plague. While he yet spake, there came from the ruler of the synagogue's house certain which said, Thy daughter is dead: why troublest thou the Master any further? As soon as Jesus heard the word that was spoken, he saith unto the ruler of the synagogue, Be not afraid, only believe."

Our Lord's unhurrying delay here, to single out and speak to that anonymous woman who had touched the fringe of His robe, would seem exasperatingly needless and unsympathetic to the overwrought father of the dying girl. Synagogue-ruler Jairus must have been agonized by the fear that while our Lord lingered the life of his dying child was fast ebbing away. Our Lord not only took time to hear some of the thronging people deny having touched

Him, and time to wait for the woman to confess, but with no sense of hurry He tarried to pronounce a blessing upon her in the hearing of the crowd. The anxious father's fear, alas, was confirmed. While Jesus still lingered, speaking to the woman, messengers came from the house of the synagogue ruler to say that any further appeal to Jesus was of no use; the little maid had died. To that broken-hearted father the delay must have been tantalizing. Had he not told Jesus that it was a matter of only minutes if his child was to be snatched from death? Jesus could have got there, just in the nick of time, if only He had not aggravatingly lingered with the crowd and that woman! Yes, the delay did seem strange.

But now we turn to what is perhaps the strangest delay of all, that is, our Lord's delay before going to Bethany after learning that Lazarus was ill. The Lazarus episode is related in the eleventh chapter of John, and is so well known that we scarcely need quote at length from it. But note carefully again what is said about the delay in verses 5, 6 and 7.

"Now Jesus loved Martha, and her sister, and Lazarus. When He had heard therefore that Lazarus was sick, He abode two days still in the same place where He was. Then after that He saith to His disciples, Let us go into Judaea again."

There is a strange-seeming deliberateness about our Lord's delay here which marks it off from the other two delays. His delay in going to the storm-tossed disciples might be put down in some degree to His preoccupation in prayer; and His delay on the way to heal Jairus's daughter might be extenuatingly excused on the ground that He halted to confer healing on another sufferer who had just as much claim upon Him as the little girl. But here, in connection with Lazarus, the delay is deliberate. Notice that strange "therefore" in verse 6. "Now Jesus loved

83

Martha and her sister and Lazarus . . . therefore when He had heard that Lazarus was sick He abode two days . . . where He was." It seemed a contradictory way of showing love! Plainly, Lazarus's illness was considered dangerous. Otherwise the sisters would not have sent for our Lord to come; for Bethany was near Jerusalem, where quite recently the Jews had tried to stone Jesus, as the sisters well knew. Evidently Martha and Mary were anxious. Yet although our Lord had such special love for them and for Lazarus, He deliberately delayed for those two days! And, as we gather from verses 7 and 11, it was just at the end of those two days that Lazarus died! Bethabara beyond Jordan was about two days distance by foot to Bethany; so our Lord could have got there before illness gave place to death. Moreover, even after those two days, He evidently lingered on the journey, for when He reached Bethany Lazarus had already been four days in the tomb (the entombing presumably having taken place on the day of demise, according to Palestinian custom). Certainly, the delay would seem strange to Martha and Mary—very strange indeed.

THEIR INWARD PURPOSE

Well, such was the outward strangeness of those three delays. Let us now look at them a little more closely, to see their inward purpose.

The first thing which becomes obvious is that those delays simply had to be as they were, in order to demonstrate our Lord's supreme power in a never-to-be-forgotten way. In the first incident there had to be delay till the storm had lasted long enough for those storm-battered boatmen to become beaten and baffled by it. Only so would they realize in the intended way our Lord's uttermost power over Nature. (See Matt. 14:33, Mark 6:52.) In the second incident there had to be delay long enough for the dread news to come to Jairus that the worst had happened; that the little one was actually dead. Only so could our Lord demonstrate His power, not only over disease, but even over death.

In the third incident our Lord must delay long enough for the body of Lazarus to have started decomposing. Only thus could our Lord make it clear that at the resurrection of Lazarus his very soul was being recalled from Sheol or Hades to reinhabit the restored body.

Thus, through those three delays, our Lord Jesus was able to demonstrate with classic finality His power over Nature and over Death and Hades.

But besides this, a further purpose of those delays was to develop the faith of the disciples. In connection with the first delay, hear our Lord's words to Peter, "O thou of little faith, wherefore didst thou doubt?" In connection with the second delay, hear His words to Jairus, "Be not afraid; only believe." In connection with the third delay, hear His words to Martha, "Said I not unto thee that if thou wouldst believe thou shouldst see the glory of God?"

After that first delay, would those disciples ever forget the ghost-like Figure treading down the very waves? After that second delay, would Jairus ever forget our Lord's words, "Talitha cumi"? After that third delay, would the spectators ever forget the death-conquering shout of Jesus into the mouth of the dark tomb, "Lazarus, come forth"?

There may have been other purposes, too, in those three delays, but all I stay to point out here is, that in each case there was new exhibition of our Lord's sovereign power; and a new lesson on faith; a new revelation of the divine, and a new education of the human; a new demonstration that often the disciples' direst extremity is the Master's truest opportunity. This brings me to my final observation concerning those three delays of Jesus, namely:

THEIR LASTING MESSAGE

The first big object-lesson in them is that our Lord can transform the most hopeless circumstances. See the extreme plight of those disciples in that storm. They had rowed three hours, from 6 p.m. until 9, and seen daylight turn to stormy dusk. They had toiled another three hours, 9 o'clock till 12 midnight, and seen stormy dusk become tempestuous night. They had struggled yet another three hours in blackness and howling storm. Strength was exhausted; the storm was unabating; oars were now useless; and where were they? The Sea of Galilee is roughly twelve miles north to south and about six east to west; so if they had gone about three miles they were now right in the middle, at the spasm-centre of the storm, in thick darkness, with their strength petered out. Could the circumstances have seemed more hopeless?

Similarly, when the pallid-faced young daughter of Jairus had become a motionless corpse on her couch, could the situation have seemed more hopeless? When dead Lazarus had lain enwrapped by rigid embalmings four days in a sepulcher, could the situation have seemed more hopeless? Yet in each case it was at hopeless zero-point that our Lord, the Master of surprises, suddenly turned disaster into deliverance, tragedy into triumph, sighing into singing, and deepest mystery into highest meaning.

Christian believer, take this precious fact to heart; keep it gratefully in mind; it can steady you and comfort you amid many "an horror of great darkness" (Gen. 15:12). No situation is "too far gone" for our all-controlling Lord to overrule and transform. I have experienced this at unforgettable crises in my own life. When the very "sentence of death" has been written (as it would seem) at the very point of "no hope" the Lord has silently but surely brought light out of darkness, joy out of sorrow, pearls out of tears, even as Samson's bees brought honey out of the lion's carcass. Do I address someone even now who is in deep problem almost to the point of despair? Take heart! Though things seem to have gone beyond "redemption-point", though you seem to be in the swift current just above the falls, though you cannot figure out how even God could alter things for you now except by ending the world's history, He knows better than you. He is the Master-Planner of eleventh-hour deliverances. Let both Scripture and the voice of Christian experience convince you that again and again the blackest sky has been suddenly enringed by the brightest rainbow; the weeping willow has become the victory-palm; and the "dews of sorrow" have suddenly become lustrous with precious evidences of Heaven's loving-kindness!

> I know not by what methods rare,
> But this I know, God answers prayer:
> I know that He has given His word,
> Which pledges prayer is always heard,
> And will be answered, soon or late;
> So let me pray and calmly wait.
>
> I know not if the blessing sought
> Will come in just the way I thought;
> I leave my prayer with Him alone
> Whose will is wiser than my own;
> Assured that He will grant my quest,
> Or send an answer far more blest.

But, now, another reassuring lesson which we learn from those delays of Jesus is, that our greatest discoveries and blessings often come through our sorest trials. When our Lord walked across the waves to that rocking boat, not only did the storm thereupon subside into gentle calm, but, as John 6:21 says, "Immediately the ship was at the land whither they went". Our Lord's delayed answers are always the quickest way to blessing. In the case of Jairus, not only did he meet Jesus the healer, but suddenly he discovered himself face to face with "God who raiseth the dead" (2 Cor. 1:9). As for the raising of Lazarus, the biggest discovery and joy of their life came thereby to Martha and Mary. They had already entertained the dearest thoughts of Jesus; but now, at one and the same time, they saw the most touching evidence of His humanness as He "wept" at their brother's grave, and the most overpowering evidence of His deity as He proved Himself "the Resurrection and the Life"!

Tired and troubled Christian, beware of thinking that God is harsh as you drag along amid permitted sorrow or tribulation. It is easy, when the mind is tortured by suffering or tensed by pain, to attribute fantastic ugliness to God. How His great father-heart must be grieved by this! If only we could grasp this fact: it is His permitting and overruling of calamities which leads to our most exalting and refining discoveries! Let Robert W. Service's lines bear witness to that fact:

> I sought Him on the purple seas;
>   I sought Him on the peaks aflame;
> Amid the gloom of giant trees
>   And canyons lone, I called His name.
> The wasted ways of earth I trod;
> In vain! In vain! I found not God.
>
> I sought Him in the lives of men,
>   In cities grand, in hamlets grey,
> In temples old beyond our ken,
>
>   And tabernacles of today.
> All life I sought from cloud to clod.
> In vain! In vain! I found not God.
>
> Then, after roaming far and wide,
>   In streets and seas and deserts wild,
> I came at last to stand beside
>   The death-bed of my little child.
> Lo, as I bent beneath the rod,
> I raised my eyes . . . and there was GOD!

A final lesson which comes to us is, that in divine delays there is always a gracious purpose. Our Lord could do no other than wait until those storm-tossed disciples had come to an end of self-struggling. Equally so, He had to let the little girl die if His bigger purpose was to be fulfilled. Again, it was altogether necessary that Lazarus should be dead and buried a full four days so that a competent number of witnesses might have time to gather; also in order that both the death and the resurrection-miracle might be indisputable facts even to hostile observers. The delay, with its seeming lack of tenderness toward the mourning sisters, was needful because wider interests than those of a single family were involved. In each of those long-ago delays of Jesus there was a rich and gracious purpose.

Dear fellow-believer, try to learn this truth deeply: there is always gracious purpose in divine delays toward you. Try to remember this: delay does not mean that God is neglecting you, much less that He has forsaken you. Be persuaded of this, also, that delayed answer to your prayer does not mean denial of your prayer. How readily many of us jump to the drastic conclusion that God has said, "No," when in truth He has said nothing! Do I need to remind you that there is a big difference between saying, "No," and saying nothing? A young fellow asks his father for a sum of money which, so he says, he urgently needs. If the father plainly says, "No," that settles it; but if he says nothing the son waits hopefully. If a young man asks a young woman to marry him, and she replies a definite "No", that settles it; but if she says nothing his heart still flutters with hope.

We should try to realize that if God's highest purposes for us are to be effected, delays in granting our prayers are often necessary. Sometimes, in our own hearts, there are unsuspected hindrances which need to be removed before there can be a safe "Yes" to us. As I myself now look back over some of the prayers I have prayed, how glad I am that God did not say "Yes"! (Do not others of you feel the same?). It was not always that God said a direct "No" to me, but there first had to be inward tutoring, discipline, sanctification, guidance, to make the "yes" safe—and that meant time, process, delay. A box of matches is very useful to mother in the kitchen; but don't give it to that rascally young child unless you want the house on fire! That sharp knife is very useful to daddy; but don't give it to that little boy who is crying for it, unless you want him to hurt himself! Try to remember, dear Christian, God has a plan for you, as well as your own! His is always safe and best for you: yours may be otherwise! The thing which you want most could be the most dangerous!

There is one other thing I would add. Sometimes God may say, "Yes"; sometimes He may say "No", He may answer by delay—a delay with a bigger blessing in view than either an immediate "Yes" or an immediate "No" could confer. But this is certain: no sincere prayer in the Name of Jesus is ever left unanswered; and delay is always with a view to an answer bigger and better than that for which we asked.

Ungranted yet, the prayer your lips have pleaded
   In agony of heart these many years?
Does faith begin to fail, is hope departing?
   And think you all in vain your falling tears?
Say not the Father has not heard your prayer;
Full answer there shall be, sometime, somewhere.

Ungranted yet? Though when you first presented
   This one petition at the Father's throne,
It seemed you could not wait the time of asking
   So urgent was your heart to make it known:
Though years have passed, pray on, do not despair,
Such prayer must answered be, sometime, somewhere.

Ungranted yet? Nay, do not say, "unanswered";
   Perhaps your part is not yet wholly done;
The work began when first your prayer was uttered
   And God will finish what He has begun.
If you still keep the incense burning there,
His answer you shall see, sometime, somewhere!

Ungranted yet? Faith cannot be unanswered:
  Her feet are firmly planted on the Rock;
Amid the wildest storm she stands undaunted,
  Nor quails amid the loudest thunder shock.
She moves Omnipotence to hear her prayer
And cries it shall be done, sometime, somewhere!

A certain godly couple had three boys, and brought
them up in the Christian faith. They not only prayed for
them, they prayed with them, teaching them the habit of
prayer. Yet as those three lads grew up into healthy youths
they did not share or profess any such godliness as that of
their parents. Then their mother died, but the father kept
on praying for them and with them. He always gathered
them round him for family prayers at an old, cane-seated
chair; and oh, what prayers he prayed for them, kneeling at
that old, cane-seated chair! Eventually the father himself
died—when the three sons were grown men, all very successful in business, but never having made any Christian
profession. After the funeral the three sons came back to
settle what should be done about the furniture and other
matters. One of them suggested, "Let's give these things to
the elderly woman who has been looking after father." The
eldest brother replied, "Well, I'm quite agreeable, except for
this: I would like to have that old, cane-bottomed chair.
I never heard prayers like those which dear dad prayed
for us at that chair." As he spoke his voice trembled, and
tears were in his eyes. Neither could the other two brothers
conceal their emotion. Then the eldest brother said, "Let's
kneel down again at that old, cane-bottomed chair." They
did so; and one said to another, "If I had to live my life over
again, I would not live without prayer and without God."
Tears flowed; and there, at that old, cane-seated chair, all
three brothers gave themselves to Christ. Two of them left
business and went abroad as Christian missionaries, and the
other brother, also, became a fervent public servant of the
Lord. Neither the mother nor the father lived on earth to

91

see the answer to their prayers; but the answer came—and somehow I think they knew up in heaven.

Dear Christian, buffeted by the billows, or praying with tears over smarting problems, and downcast by this puzzle of divine delay, be comforted. The God who bled to save you on Calvary loves you too well ever to mock you! Can you be more dismayed than the poet William Cowper must have been by his recurrent mental affliction? Yet it was he who glimpsed the sun-shaft through the draping gloom, and wrote,

> Ye fearful saints, fresh courage take!
>   The clouds ye so much dread
> Are big with mercy, and shall break
>   In blessings on your head!
>
> Blind unbelief is sure to err,
>   And scan God's work in vain;
> God is His own interpreter,
>   And He will make it plain.

Matthew and Mark and John all tell us that when our Lord walked the waves and drew near to the scared disciples, His first word which rang out to them across the waters was, "Be of good cheer! It is I; be not afraid!" He comes to you, this very day, across the troubled waters of your wondering and questioning. He calls to you now, not just from the New Testament page, but in your innermost consciousness,

"BE OF GOOD CHEER! IT IS I;
BE NOT AFRAID!"[7]

six

#####

THE MOVE ACROSS
THE ATLANTIC

Now the LORD had said unto Abram, Get thee out of thy
country, and from thy kindred, and from thy father's house,
unto a land that I will shew thee.

GENESIS 12:1

His Expanding Ministry

During the early 1950s the Baxters began to travel more
and more abroad. Baxter was a frequent guest lecturer at
Christian conferences in Canada and America. And it wasn't
long before he and Ethel realized that broader ministry op-
portunities lay across the Atlantic Ocean. His books were
becoming more accessible to the American public and word

soon "got out" about the uniqueness of this English gentleman who so eloquently preached God's Word.

Once an audience got a taste of J. Sidlow Baxter's ingra-
tiating personality and his booming articulate voice, they
wanted to hear more of him. So repeat offers to preach
at churches, conferences, and seminaries flooded in. His
ministry was expanding far more than he could ever realize. Seminary students in Canada and America were soon
discussing his books. And congregations were challenged
by his prophetic messages. Pastors were being influenced
by his deep conviction of the necessity of churches to return
to the roots of Christian worship through the older hymns
and expository preaching.

This expanding ministry began on May 29, 1949, at
a church meeting; Pastor Baxter announced to his office
bearers the need for him to answer the pressing invitations abroad to preach. He also wanted to tour the mission
field and visit the church's own missionaries. The church
agreed unanimously and he and Ethel were off to travel
distant shores. Sid soon realized the vastness of ministry
opportunity abroad. He was also beginning to hear that
"still small voice" in his spirit leading him to move per-
manently to the United States. But his heart was wed to
the dear members of Charlotte Chapel—it was his home.
How could he leave them? A singular incident decided
the matter for him.

For a better understanding of the incident, a history lesson in the emotions of the Scots is appropriate. C. H. Spurgeon found out about the reserved behavior of the Scottish
people when he first preached in Scotland in 1855 at the
age of twenty-one. He wrote in his journal,

> After prayer and singing I began to preach; but there were
> no eyes of fire, and no beaming countenances, to cheer
> me while proclaiming the gospel message. The greater

part of the congregation sat in apparent indifference; they seemed made of lumps of ice. I tried all means to move them, but in vain . . . I felt like the Welshman who could make Welshmen jump, but could not move the English. I thought within myself, "Surely your blood is very cold here, for everywhere else I should have seen signs of emotion while preaching Christ and Him crucified." Feeling rather sad at our singular service, I went into the street, and was delighted to find that, although cold as marble in the building, they were now hearty and full of feeling.[1]

The reserved emotions of the Scots make the following incident so dramatic. Upon returning to Edinburgh, Sid and Ethel walked up the stairs to the chapel of their beloved church to find the following: banners were strung atop the balcony and signs were hanging from the half-moon pulpit that read, "We love you! Welcome back! We love our dear Pastor!" The overt display of emotion brought tears to Sid's and Ethel's eyes. But something of the moment disturbed Sid and he couldn't quite put his finger on it right away. It bothered him later in the day and he remarked to his wife, "My dear, it is time for us to go from here. For the people are beginning to worship me rather than the Lord."[2]

In 1952 Rev. Baxter resigned as pastor but stayed until February 1953 to celebrate (at the office-bearers' request) his semijubilee in the ministry. The Baxters remained in Edinburgh until 1955, when they finally decided to move abroad. So it was with departing tears that they set sail for America.

It was a bittersweet good-bye to bonny Scotland and those he had so dearly loved. He recounts the moment in his book *Rethinking Our Priorities.*

On the first day of January, 1955, my dear wife and I left Liverpool, England, for our eighth visit to the U.S.A. and

Canada. I had now resigned from my eighteen-year pastorate in Edinburgh, Scotland, and was venturing forth on a wider ministry of itinerant Bible teaching. It felt strange to be making such a break from our British moorings, but we felt sure of divine guidance; so, in the words of Paul, we "thanked God and took courage".

It was our thought to spend two years in America, then to move on to engagements in New Zealand, Australia, South Africa, India, and Japan. Little did we foresee that our two years in America would lengthen indefinitely! Let me pay grateful tribute to the many evangelical ministers who, with their churches, have warmly welcomed us and responded to our ministry of the Word. Everywhere we have been received with cordiality.[3]

Sid and Ethel would travel all forty-eight states on the mainland and eventually settle in California. California, with its mountain and ocean views, reminded Sid of England—only the weather was much more agreeable!

His Home in Santa Barbara

The coastal community of Santa Barbara is a jewel on the California Riviera. The city, smallish with a population of around 90,000, has come a long way from life in a one-room adobe with a wooden lean-to. Horses and grist mills have been replaced with noisy traffic and bustling commerce. Hollywood mansions dot the hillsides and the seaside community much resembles the Amalfi coast and the isle of Capri.[4]

The city is rich with history as well. Back when California was a wilderness frontier, the Spanish built a chain of four military fortresses along the coast. In 1782, the Santa Barbara Royal Presidio was the last in a chain of four. The

Sid at his home in Santa Barbara, California

presidio played a strategic role in the occupation of New Spain and, as a fortress, protected the settlers against attacks by local Indians, as well as guarded the country from foreign invaders. This Spanish-Mexican heritage can still be felt today.

The sunny California coastline has for many years attracted both poets and writers. From Robert Louis Stevenson to John Steinbeck, California has been a haven for creative types. It was here in the land of sun and surf that J. Sidlow Baxter would spend the second half of his life. Though his earlier poems and books, such as *The Hidden Hand* and *Explore the Book*, were written in England and Scotland, much of his large body of work was penned during the Santa Barbara years. Most of the books were written in the home by the beach that Sid shared with his first wife, Ethel. However, during the twenty years at Skyview Drive, where he lived with his second wife, Isabella, such works as

97

Daily Wings and *The Other Side of Death* were pounded out on his old manual typewriter, the keys worn from overuse. He also wrote many poems, hymns, and three unpublished manuscripts.

After logging many miles on frequent-flier tickets to itinerant preaching engagements, the Baxters found solace and refuge among the craggy cliffs and sloshing waves of the Pacific Ocean. However, during the forty-plus years that Sid worked and lived in Santa Barbara, the majority of the residents took little notice of the British gentleman who strolled the beaches with a pensive look about him. Baxter, as he walked, shared companionship with Jehovah in the same manner as Abraham of old. And this same Jehovah would have trials and tests for his servant in California, just as he did for the patriarch of Israel. However, God would bestow many blessings for faithfulness as well.

Sid and Ethel landed for good in Santa Barbara and called it home. Sid's sister Eunice also was nearby, having settled there with her family. The town of Santa Barbara has a European flair to it unlike many other American cities. Baxter felt comfortable in the small community, and the warmer climate suited him. Though he never became an American citizen, insisting to the end that he was always an Englishman, he would proudly call California home. Santa Barbara would hold many joys and many tears for him.

He did not realize it at the time, but he was a very sick man. An episode was to occur that would bring him again to the throes of death.

seven

THE ILLNESS
AND THE HEALING

> And a woman having an issue of blood twelve years, which
> had spent all her living upon physicians, neither could be
> healed of any, came behind him, and touched the border of
> his garment: and immediately her issue of blood stanched.
>
> LUKE 8:43–44

The Grand Climacteric

In 1966, in the city of Santa Barbara, California, lay a
very sick patient in a darkened room at Cottage Hospital.
Acute diabetes had made the patient critically ill, near to
the point of coma and death. Although the staff doctors
had little hope for the patient's recovery (at the very best
a life kept in private as an invalid), a force was working
behind the scenes. While J. Sidlow Baxter lay seemingly at

99

the point of death, God was preparing to make a hospital visit to his faithful servant. He had laid Sid low to speak to him. And speak he did. On a fog-laden morning in Santa Barbara, the Divine Presence came down in the form of a vision to this prophet of God.

In his book *Divine Healing of the Body*, he recounts the incident in surprising detail.

How can I ever forget those two weeks in that hospital! Something happened there which I could never have guessed beforehand. The Lord met me and did something new in my life.

As soon as I entered, of course, I was given insulin treatment; and careful tests were taken daily. True enough, I had become badly diabetic. The tests confirmed it. But by this time I had resignedly leaned my weary head on my heavenly Father's bosom. I had wrestled my heart into complete surrender to His permissive will for me. I knew that the God who bled for me on Calvary could never mock me, that He was sympathetically sharing with me, and that He would somehow overrule to my eternal good the calamity which He had allowed to lay me low. And He did. Let me tell you about it.

When I was just a young Christian, in my late teens and early twenties, I used to envy those Christians who testified to having "visions from the Lord." It seemed to me that theirs must be a superior, aerified kind of spirituality. As time slipped by, however, I revised my thinking. Observation caused me to suspect that in most cases the visions were a product of excitable imagination; for apparently they served no real purpose and tended to beget a dreamy kind of religion rather than solid Christian character. At any rate, I myself have never been the type to have visions. I considered it extremely unlikely that ever the Lord would speak to me by such a means, but while I was in the hospital that is just what He did!

Either, the second or third morning, when I was emerging from sleep into that hazy semiconsciousness before one becomes fully awake, I had a vision. There was a bright amber background, then, in the forefront, a Bible—opened to Psalm 103; and next a hand appeared with the index finger pointing to verse 3: "who forgiveth all thine iniquities."

What those words conveyed to me at that moment I could hardly get over to you vividly enough. They seemed to say, "Sid, what does it matter basically whether you live or die, whether you are well or ill, compared with knowing that you are saved, that you have a full, free, final, and forever forgiveness, a forgiveness which is not merely a pardon but a loving welcome to the heavenly Father's heart, and that you have a ministry for Him in that fair realm beyond the grave?"

"Who forgiveth all thine iniquities"—the words were like a glistening rainbow overarching me all that day.

The next morning, just at the same time and in the same way, there again was the same vision the amber background, the Bible opened to Psalm 103, and the hand with the pointing index finger. But now the finger moved to the next clause in the psalm: "Who healeth all thy diseases." Never had those words seemed so wonderful. They stood out with a neon glow. I looked and looked and looked. They were before my inner eyes all day. I knew, I knew, I knew: God was about to heal me!

The third morning, there it all was again: the amber background, the Bible opened to Psalm 103, and the pointing hand; but now the finger had moved to the further clause: "So that thy youth is renewed like the eagle's." Even as I came out of the vision, I was still overcome with wonder. I knew that God was telling me not only that He was going to heal me but that I was going to be renewed into even better health than ever hitherto. I recalled that the eagle is a long-lived bird and that (besides its annual molting) when it is near a hundred years old, it casts all its feathers, from head to talons, and has a complete re-feathering. So far as I know, the eagle is unique in that respect; and that, of course, is why the psalmist used it for his illustration: "Thy youth is renewed like the eagle's."

As I kept looking at the promise, something else flashed into my mind. In a lecture which I had recently prepared, I had made a point of the difference between a "climacteric" and a "climax." My dictionary definition of a climacteric is "A period or point in human life in which some great change in the constitution of health takes place." Just underneath it adds, "The Grand Climacteric: the sixty-third year; supposed to be a critical year for men"! And there I was, in my sixty-third year! It was my "grand climacteric" all right!—and God was meeting me then in a strangely wonderful way, with forgiving love, healing power, and gracious health renewal! He had laid me low that He might lift me up reconditioned for new service.

Soon "signs" began to appear. During the hours following the second vision, I had insulin shock; that is, my blood sugar level suddenly dropped from way, way up down to the low fifties. One of the doctors was called. From then on my insulin injection was reduced. Two days later my sugar level plummeted again. The doctors were puzzled. The insulin injections were further readjusted.

Some days later I left the hospital, with diet charts, insulin gadgets, and instruction booklet; but deep down I knew they would not be needed. Nor were they. The Lord had told me He wanted me to do another ten years of travel ministry. During all those ten years there was no recurrence of the trouble.[1]

Dr. Baxter's travel ministry did not end in 1976, ten years after this incident. His last travel preaching date was in 1991—at the age of eighty-eight! Even then he was youthful, energetic, and amazing. It makes one think of the re-feathering of the long-lived eagle when it nears one hundred years old. A sovereign God keeps his promises to his people.

J. Sidlow Baxter was two months shy of his ninety-seventh birthday when at last God refeathered him for his heavenly homecoming.

Ethel's Cancer

The Greek Isles, steeped in a history intertwined with myth and fact, are a paradox. Set like white diamonds in a ring of Aegean green, their visual similarity is contradicted by their distinguishable dissimilarity. The Greek islands (like offspring of the same parents) stand in contrast to their other siblings. Mykonos, dotted with white limestone buildings, is the wild child. With lazy pelicans and softly turning windmills, this carefree island yields itself to one's libido.

On the other hand, Patmos, with its fortresslike monastery of Saint John, which stands atop the highest peak, represents the pious child who is silent in religious worship. While the tourists to Mykonos can indulge their wildest fantasies with no thought to cost, the monks at Patmos live in total privation with little thought to the flesh. And in this beautiful little chain of islands in the Aegean Sea, one's emotions can swing from the highest of highs to the lowest of lows.

It was late 1973 when the Baxters returned home to sunny Santa Barbara, exhausted from a tour of Greece and the Aegean islands. Though physically tired, Sid's spirits were high from the lectures he had given to eager audiences and the thrill of retracing the steps of both the apostle Paul and apostle John. Yet, as a surreptitious band of darkening clouds suddenly cover the sun, his high emotions crashed like California waves against bleak rocks below. Ethel had bad news for him. Cancer.

In his book *Divine Healing of the Body*, Sid details the terrible news.

We had been home only a few days when my wife said, "Sid, I have disturbing news for you: I have cancer." I could scarcely believe my ears; but she had indeed said it, and her grave look told me that she really meant it.

"Oh, Ethel, are you quite sure? If so, how long have you known?—and why did you not tell me sooner?"

"Yes, I'm pretty sure. I knew it well before we went on the tour, but I did not want it to interfere with your ministry."

The very next day I accompanied her to our doctor. As soon as he saw the evidence he groaned, "Oh, Mrs. Baxter, this certainly seems like cancer. Let me call in the surgeon at once; he is only a couple of doors away." One look by the surgeon was enough to confirm it; and his big regret was that the growth had apparently now traveled right into the armpit and the lymph system. There and then a date was fixed for the operation—mastectomy, for metastic carcinoma.

As we came out from our interview with the surgeon my mind was dazed. I felt as though I would fall to pieces, for it seemed a foregone conclusion that I was to lose my lifelong companion. Her father had died of cancer. So had her eldest brother. So had her next-younger brother. My Ethel and I had been little neighbors when we were only a few years old. We had grown up together. We had gone to the same school. She had never had any sweetheart but me and I none but her. Our union of heart and memory went right back to early childhood. The thought of the dark, empty blank without her was dismaying beyond words. I knew the Lord would somehow prove all-sufficient, and there was no rebellion in my heart; but I was all too human, and it seemed to me as though the sun was suddenly being blotted out of my sky.

The date of the operation was December 12, 1973. My dear one braved it trustfully and survived it successfully. In fact she healed from the surgery remarkably well. However, healing from the mastectomy was one thing: complete cure from cancer in her system was a very different matter. Bit by bit we learned afterward that there was far more and far worse.

She was put on a course of treatment by radiation. This rather surprised us and aroused our suspicion that more cancer was there, and it surely was—more than we then knew. She came through the several weeks and twenty installments of radiation with only minor accompaniments of irritation such as radiation often provokes; but, alas, there was now a paralysis of the left vocal cord which left her voiceless: even whispers were a struggle.

By that time another worrying symptom was her rapid loss of weight. She was becoming a mere shadow of her former healthy womanhood. Along with that, it was cutting to my own heart to see in her that strange fear which so often grips the cancer victim.

It was decided by the doctors that she should be put on a chemotherapy course of treatment, i.e., on a hormonal and chemical therapy program. But as a prior requirement to that they arranged for an operation on her vocal cord. We were told that the throat operation would be a "quite minor" one and that Mrs. Baxter could probably leave the hospital in the evening of the same day.

Instead of leaving the hospital the same day, she came the nearest to dying (so it seemed) that she had ever been and had to remain in the hospital some days. She started having gagging spasms. She could scarcely swallow either solids or liquids; and if the slightest speck of anything got on the trachea (windpipe), she would choke, unable to breathe. Apparently the radiation had so dried her up inside that the chest and throat muscles did not have normal flexibility to expand and contract. As the surgeon said, "Even at best, radiation is a mixed blessing." It was awful to see my dear one suffer so. Ten or a dozen times during those days I held her in my arms during critical chokings, expecting any second to be her last.

Then came the chemotherapy. I am only stating what everyone now knows when I say that the drugs used in chemotherapy are lethal. That is the very word the doctor himself used in telling me about them—"lethal." She was put on Stilbestrol, Cytoxan, and weekly intravenous injections of Fluorouracil and Methotrexate. From the start there were distressing side effects which I will not here describe, but what alternative to chemotherapy was there?

One day I chatted with the doctor for a few minutes, in Ethel's absence. "Will this treatment cure her?" He slowly shook his head and then explained that there was a whole cancer "mass" in her mediastinum (the space between the lungs) and that there were cancerous nodes up the left lung. It was quite inoperable. Attempted surgical removal would kill her.

"How long has she?" I asked him. He paused, then slowly replied, "Eight months, maybe; or it could possibly be a couple of years."

I knew then that there had either to be a miracle or a funeral. Up to that point, although I had prayed fervently that God would heal and restore Ethel, I had meant that He would use the surgery and other natural means to do so. But now, since all such earthly skills were confessedly impotent, I was cast on God alone for supernatural intervention. Day after day, early and late, I sought the dear heavenly Master whom for fifty years I had loved, adored, and preached. I knew that many others were praying as well. Yet somehow I could not find Him in the way I needed and wondered why He should seem so distant.

Then, very early one morning, about three weeks after my special praying had started, He was there, in my study! I knew it. He was really there. I did not see Him—yet I did! Many of you will know what I mean. As clearly as could be, He said to me in deep-down heart language, "All right, Sid. You think I have not been listening; but I have. I know your need of Ethel. I have kept you waiting for a purpose which you will soon know. Sid, if you can take it in simple faith, the healing is yours."

Ethel Baxter, Northampton, England

Yes, I knew instantaneously that He had said it; and amid my tears of grief and joy, in simple faith I "took" it. That instant, though neither Ethel nor I had the slightest physical evidence of it then, the whole cancer mass disappeared—as was verified two days later.

The second day after that early morning experience, we had to be at the doctor's for the weekly examination. As it was the seventh such, she had to have another X-ray that day, along with special clinical tests to check on what side effects the chemotherapy drugs might be having. The first inkling that anything inside Ethel had happened was when the doctor saw the blood report. He glanced at it, then picked up his phone and said, "No, that's Mrs. Baxter's." After that Ethel went with him and a lady doctor into another room for the clinical examination.

So far as I can recall, it was some ten to fifteen minutes later that the doctor came to me in the waiting room and said something like this: "Well! Dr. Baxter, I would like to have a chat with you about your wife, but I cannot stay now as I am due in the theater for surgery. We are certainly surprised—very pleased, of course, but puzzled. That large cancer mass about which I told you and the cancer nodes up the left lung—they have all completely gone! My colleague will show you the X-ray taken some seven weeks ago and the new one taken this morning."

Well, we saw the two X-rays side by side, and there was no mistaking: the new one was thoroughly clear! Can you imagine our feelings? We wept, we sang, we praised, we winged hosannas to heaven. I was back in Psalm 30.

> O LORD my God, I cried unto thee,
>   And thou hast healed me.
> Thou hast turned for me my mourning
>   Into dancing;
> Thou hast put off my sackcloth,
>   And girded me with gladness.
>
> (PSALM 30:2, 11)[2]

As Moses had cried out to Jehovah upon Mount Sinai on behalf of his people, so the face of God was turned to hear the pleading of J. Sidlow Baxter. And as Moses had descended the mount the first time with his face aglow, fresh from being in the presence of a holy God, Sid would spend the rest of his life in utter dependence upon the one who answered him.

eight

||||||||||||||||||||||||||||||||||||||||||||||||||||||||||||||||||||||||||||||||

THE GRIEF
AND THE LOSS

And Rachel died, and was buried in the way to Ephrath,
which is Bethlehem. And Jacob set a pillar upon her grave:
that is the pillar of Rachel's grave unto this day.

GENESIS 35:19–20

Till Death Do Us Part

As the mutable Mississippi River quietly courses its way
from Memphis to New Orleans, its muddy waters leave silt
deposits along the riverbank. Over time these silt deposits
become sandbars and occasional islands. In Memphis, at
the foot of Tom Lee Park where cannons from the Civil
War still stand guard, there lies an entire island called Mud
Island—born from these steady muddy deposits.

The Memphis preaching engagements of J. Sidlow Baxter, beginning in 1977 and continuing until 1991, had steadily left siltlike deposits in the hearts of those who heard him expound God's Word. And with each new preaching engagement, he deposited more and more blessings that eventually grew into an island of joy for those who heard him.

It was late February 1977, when the Baxters arrived in the river town. Sid and Ethel were in Memphis at the request of Dr. Adrian Rogers, pastor of the huge Bellevue Baptist Church. Baxter's writings had impacted the ministry of Adrian Rogers, so Dr. Rogers had asked Baxter to come. Dr. Rogers, then president of the large body of Southern Baptists, had taken the convention by storm. Adrian Rogers was part of a group of conservative leaders whose stance on the literal interpretation of Scripture eventually changed the balance of power among Southern Baptists. Adrian Rogers's prominence had roused Sid's curiosity and was one of the reasons Sid agreed to come to Memphis to preach. Straightway, Adrian Rogers and J. Sidlow Baxter became friends.

Sid and Ethel checked into their hotel room in downtown Memphis. A demanding schedule lay ahead. From February 27 to March 2 he was to hold daily meetings, often preaching two to three times a day—all at the age of seventy-four!

One luncheon meeting where Sid preached is still talked about at Bellevue Baptist to this day. It was a businessmen's luncheon in the cafeteria of the church. Normally, the speaker preached while the people ate. However, that day it was different. The Spirit of God was upon Sid like a cloak. As he began to preach, the people hushed. One by one they laid down their knives and forks to hear what he was saying. As Sid continued to preach about the love of Jesus, revival broke out in that cafeteria.

Sid and Ethel retired to their hotel room at the end of each day, exhausted. He was tired from the heavy preaching schedule. She was tired for another reason. Little did the long-married couple know this was to be one of the last times she would accompany her husband. Ethel's exhaustion was due to failing health.

Ethel, his childhood sweetheart. Ethel, his life companion. Ethel, his colaborer in ministry. Ethel, his queen—dying of the cancer which had befallen her four years earlier. Sid preached his heart out at those long Bellevue meetings, but his poor heart was soon to break.

All Alone

There are some things in life which will always remain a mystery, at least on this side of heaven. The Trinity is one. The virgin birth of Christ another. So also is the unexpected death of a loved one.

Ethel Baxter died in Santa Barbara in 1977. Sid's life journey with her had abruptly ended. The normally edenic California sky became as gray to him as a cold London day.

For the next two years he paced around his little home by the beach, wishing he could hear her footsteps once more. Wishing he could hear her laugh once more. Hoping he could survive the loss of his beloved queen. He could not vanquish the loneliness.

He talks about that tender time in his life in his book *Divine Healing of the Body*.

> How can I tell you? In one of his strangest-seeming providences, our dear Lord allowed my precious Ethel to suffer weariness and pain for some days and then took her to be with himself in the heavenly home, only four years after her wonderful healing.

How we had loved each other through the years! At the time of her translation we were just about to celebrate our golden wedding anniversary. Right through our long wedlock our love for each other had grown not only deeper but fonder. I can truthfully say that to the very end my dear queen never walked into my study but I thrilled. And now (oh, grief beyond expression) she was gone, inexorably gone, never to walk again from room to room in our dear little home. To think of her yonder, actually looking into the face of Jesus, seeing "the King in his beauty," living in the transfiguring radiance of his face, experiencing the exquisite rapture of heaven, how could I help but reverently thrill and adore, and even indulge a little envy? But here on the earthward side, oh, the pain of the parting, the sense of bereftness, the bleak blank, the stab of fear in thinking of the lonely future!

Yet I must not omit to give my testimony to this: from the time of her going our wonderful Savior became more wonderful to me than ever hitherto. He matched my emergency with his all-sufficiency. Since then, in my daily trystings with him, He has somehow been nearer, clearer, dearer, than ever before. I thought I would never sing or smile again: but He has turned my fear to faith, my sighing to singing, my grievous loss to spiritual gain, my bereftness into richer communion with Himself. He has taught me to "sing Hallelujah through my tears": and if I may reverently say so, here on earth Jesus never looks so beautiful as when we see him through our tears. It is then that we see most of all what He can be to us.

From that time onwards our Lord began to speak to me in a comforting new way through the promises and assurances of His written Word. Time would fail to tell how this and that and the other passage have leapt into brilliant new meaning. It has reminded me of something which happened when I was just a youth. One night soon after I had got into bed and was about to fall asleep I was startled by a strange, bright light underneath the bedclothes, quite near to my face. I wondered what on earth it could be. At first it seemed like two sharp, bright eyes, then it became a ring of glowing points, and then a disc of opalescent light. A moment later I chuckled to realize what it was. I had forgotten to take my wristwatch off, and it had a luminous face—that is, a face which became luminous in darkness. Oh, there are so many promises of Scripture which become luminous with new meaning in our times of darkness! That is what I found after my bereavement.

Then, as the days became weeks and months, I began to realize that there was a golden lining to the frowning cloud. I began to detect reasons why our Lord had taken my dear one. For one thing, I discerned how kind it was to my Ethel that she should have been taken first, rather than my having been taken, leaving her in widowhood—which would have been beset with trying circumstances which I will not here take space to detail. The more I reviewed the situation, the more confirmed I became that there was divine wisdom and considerateness in what had happened. There were other reasons, too, which became clear, but they are secrets between God and my own heart. I became increasingly aware, also, of God's presence enveloping me, and of his strength supporting me, and of his putting a new something into my ministry not there before. Cowper's stanzas kept singing their way into my mind:

> Ye fearful saints, fresh courage take,
>   The clouds ye so much dread,
> Are big with mercy, and shall break
>   In blessings on your head.

> Blind unbelief is sure to err,
>   And scan God's work in vain;
> God is His own interpreter,
>   And He can make it plain.[1]

114

Little did Sid know that God had another widow across the continent whose heart was broken. And sooner than Sid realized, he would journey to bonny Scotland to meet his Scottish sweetheart; and by God's grace, find a place in his heart to love again.

nine

||||||||||||||||||||||||||||||||||||||||||||||||||||||||||||||||||||||||||||||||

THE SCOTTISH
SWEETHEART

Whoso findeth a wife findeth a good thing, and obtaineth
favour of the LORD.

PROVERBS 18:22

Isabella

> My little girl in blue, dear Isa she is you.
>
> JSB

Isabella Henderson Hall was born in Munlochy, Ross-shire,
Scotland, on June 26, 1906. A blue-eyed blonde with a definite
mind and a keen sense of humor, Isa was Sid's second wife.

The story of their meeting is as amusing as it is interesting. Isa was the widow Corbett. Her first husband of forty-
four years was Roderick Corbett—a war casualty. She was
widowed in 1974. When she met J. Sidlow Baxter in 1979,

116

Isa was doing volunteer work at the local Cottage Hospital in Ross-shire. As president of the League of Friends, Isa accompanied six other volunteers on Tuesdays and Fridays to visit the hospital and perform such needed tasks as sewing or writing letters for the patients there. Isa had the heart of a servant and enjoyed helping others.

J. Sidlow Baxter came to the hospital to visit his sister-in-law, who was a patient. Upon seeing Isa, his heart was captivated by her beauty, and he admired her from afar. Though he was still grieving the loss of Ethel (who died in 1977), Sid could not keep his gaze from the woman who was to become his second wife. Soon Isa noticed the furtive glances from the dignified looking gentleman. She remarked to a friend "that there was always a man looking at me," and that this gentleman was following her. Finally, Sid got up the nerve to approach her. He asked if she would like to join him for tea and allow him to show her one of the books he had written. She flatly refused and to his dismay, politely informed him that she was not in the habit of entertaining gentleman friends.

After that encounter, Isa related the story to a relative who chastised her for treating an American visitor to their country so badly. Sid, undaunted by the first rebuff, approached her again. This time she relented, if only to show some hospitality to the kindly gentleman. Agreeing to lunch, but only if her sister-in-law could accompany them, Isa discovered they had each recently been widowed. After several such meetings, they became friends. Sid invited Isa to come to America to hear him preach in Boca Raton, Florida. Coincidentally, or perhaps divinely directed, she had already planned to visit Clearwater, Florida, to stay with friends who were there from Canada. Remarkably, this trip coincided with the time Sid would be in the Sunshine State. They agreed to meet and the courtship began.

After hearing Sid preach in Florida, it was time for Isa to return to her home in Scotland. He invited her to visit him in Santa Barbara. She agreed, since she had never been to California. Once there, she stayed at a hotel close to his home by the beach. Sid, a great believer in marriage, had made up his mind to marry her. He popped the question suddenly, "Isa, stay with me in Santa Barbara. Take care of me. Marry me."

At first she said, "No." It was time for her to be getting back to Scotland, she told him. But when she learned that her plane flight was to be canceled because of snow (again divine directive?), she decided to stay another week and think over his proposal: "I got to know Sid better then. He was taking me all over town. And again when he asked me to marry him I said, Yes."

Married Again

On April 29, 1979, Sidlow and Isabella were married in Marple, Cheshire, England. Two days after that, they returned to America and were married again in California to protect Isa from being deported. Thus began a romance that lasted twenty years.

Sid dearly loved his Scottish bride and thanked the Lord for her. They decided to move into a new house together, and Sid left the choosing to Isa, since she had a good head for financial matters and he respected her opinion. Though not as lovely as Scotland, Santa Barbara possesses a European charm, its hills dotted with houses and the Pacific Ocean below. Isa found the most delightful house atop a mountain with an ocean view. However, Sid hated it. He did not like the fireplace in the living room. Isa persisted. Sid bought the home on Skyview Drive, although he threatened to tear down the fireplace upon moving in—the fireplace remains to this day.

Sid and Isa marry on April 29, 1979, Marple, England. Isa is holding a horseshoe and Bible!

April 29, 1979, Marple, England: Sidlow and Isa with Billy and Mina Ross (Isa's brother and sister-in-law)

They took picnics on a regular basis, enjoying the out-doors and sharing cups of tea over peals of laughter. They enjoyed a good laugh and each possessed a wry sense of humor. During one picnic in Scotland, Sid had forgotten to pack a thermos, and they had no hot water for their tea. So off he went, knocking upon strangers' doors until he returned with a sheepish grin and a thermos full of boiling water! On another picnic, Sid forgot the teacups. So off he vanished once more, knocking on the doors of strangers, only to return this time with such a surprise Isa could not help howling with laughter. With his good looks, ingratiat-ing personality, and distinguished voice, he had charmed the

120

lady of the house into giving him her best china. Wedge-wood at that! Isa informed Sid if he had been a stranger coming to her home looking for cups, she certainly would not have given anything as nice as that for fear the items would never be returned. Isa always said about her husband, "Sid could charm the birds off the trees!"

They loved to take excursions together. Even though the miles of itinerant preaching often made them weary, they loved to drive up to Solvang, where they found refreshing relaxation. Sid had a radio ministry there.

Known as the Danish capital of America, Solvang, California, was founded in 1911 by Danish educators who settled there from the Midwest. The lovely Santa Ynez Valley soon was transformed by the new arrivals into a Danish village complete with windmills turning in the breeze and cottages serving smorgasbord for the growing population. It was here that J. Sidlow Baxter's booming voice was heard over FM103—a local Christian radio station. Sid's four-minute "nuggets" were heard by many appreciative listeners who often wrote him thankful letters.

Solvang, forty minutes north of Santa Barbara, was an easy drive for the Baxters. Its European atmosphere and old-world charm provided just the rest and relaxation they needed after a busy tour of preaching engagements. Usually Isa would go shopping while a studious Sid would either read in his hotel room or be found with a book by the pool. An avid reader, Sid always had a book in hand. Occasionally, Sid ventured out to buy a suit. He was especially proud of a green suit he had purchased there. Often they would go up just for the day, not staying in a hotel. On those occasions, the ever-charming Sid would act like a hotel guest and talk his way into a hotel parking lot, exclaiming to the parking attendant that he was on his way to the pool, where he would park himself at a comfortable table and begin reading a book while Isa went off to shop. "He spoke so well!" Isa would say.

Sid would usually read Isa his latest manuscript on the drive up to Solvang: She drove and he read aloud. Isa often helped him with his work, even while she was driving. Sid had a habit of using only the singular. Isa persuaded him to also use the plural to make for better reading. Having to concentrate on the road as well as her husband, Isa quipped, "It's a wonder I never killed us!"

One day, upon checking into their hotel room, Sid informed Isa he was going out for a "quick look" at the mountains. After he had been gone quite a while, Isa became concerned. She stepped out onto the hotel balcony to peer down at the street to see if she could spot her missing husband. Suddenly, she heard his voice calling to her from above where she stood. She looked up and saw Sid leaning over a balcony several floors up. Apparently, he had mistakenly entered the wrong room and, thinking Isa had gone out to shop, went outside to the balcony to get some fresh air—it was then he noticed her below, leaning over the railing looking for him. As they stood floors apart, their laughter filled the air.

They were forever laughing. For the next twenty years they shared a Christ-centered marriage.

Each day they prayed together. Each day their love for one another grew deeper. Regarding their marriage it could be truly said, "Their joys were doubled and their troubles halved."

Hearing Healed

Sid had not been feeling well when another invitation came from Dr. Adrian Rogers of Bellevue Baptist Church in 1991. He was suffering with a bad case of acid reflux, which kept him up nights and disturbed him during the day.

However, when Adrian called to invite him to "come one more time," he could not resist. Through the years, Adrian and Sid had become close friends who admired one another's preaching ability. Also, the people of Bellevue Baptist had fallen head over heels in love with Baxter. However, he wondered if he should go. Isa told him, "Go ahead, Sid. You'll be all right. God will be with you."

Few enter old age without being beset by physical maladies. Sid was no different. The acid reflux was really doing him in, for he could not keep food down and his strength was abating. The acid reflux condition went away one day a few months later. Isa was preparing dinner and left a bottle of olive oil on the dining room table. Sid poured some on his salad. It made him feel better. Every day after that for the rest of his life, he took olive oil and it cured his acid reflux. But now, in the spring of 1991, he was beset with a distressed stomach. Yet he gathered himself together for he had a message from God that he wanted to share in Memphis. It was about another physical malady—a hearing problem that God had miraculously healed. And he could not wait to tell them about that experience.

A terrible thunderstorm broke out during their flight to Memphis. The plane was going everywhere but where it should. It bounced, shuddered, rumbled, and dropped several times. Sid and Isa were sitting in first class; Isa was by the window looking out. The pilot announced that the plane was running out of fuel from being in a holding pattern and that they may have to land in a city other than Memphis. It was then that Isa heard a gasping sound. She turned to look at her beloved Sid. He was trembling. His eyes were closed and his knuckles were white as he clutched his seat's armrest. He was terrified. He would not talk to her. He cringed and gasped.

"Sid, Sid," she tried to calm him. "We will be all right."

He would not answer. Only more gasps. She had never seen a man so agitated. "Sid, Sid. Don't worry so. If we crash we'll die together. It will be all right." Still no answer. He only gasped and clutched his seat with fear. Finally, the storm passed and they were able to land safely at Memphis International Airport.

Why faith falters only Jesus knows and understands. His own followers, who were with him night and day, cried out in the midst of a storm, "Master, carest thou not that we perish? . . . And he said unto them, Why are ye so fearful? how is it that ye have no faith?" (Mark 4:38, 40). It was not that Dr. Baxter had little faith. His faith ran deep and long; his faith had stood the test of his long life. Yet he was human, as we all are.

The message that Sid preached at Bellevue Baptist the following day spoke of trusting God. He spoke of his own inability at times to fully give it all to God. The message also touched on supernatural intervention and heavenly favor. It is a remarkable sermon. Dr. Baxter was eighty-eight years old when he preached it, and not feeling well at the time. The following passage from that sermon recounts how God spoke to him one evening when he was eighty-seven years old.

Here's an experience which I recently had and which made this text unspeakably more precious to me (Philippians 4:6&7). It says you know if we commit everything to God by prayer and supplication with thanksgiving the peace of God shall guard our heart and minds. Have you ever thought about the peace of God? He had no beginning. He has no end. He never changes. He has no equal. He has no superior. His plans never go wrong. None can thwart Him. He has no enemies but those He can obliterate whenever it pleases Him. His eternity has no disturbance. His infinity has no shadow. We fluctuating transient little mortals simply cannot imagine a peace like that. That's why the text says the peace of God that passes ALL imaginings. We would have said that such an experience of having that peace would be quite impossible except that God promises it. The peace of God shall guard your hearts and minds in Christ Jesus.

Let me close by relating this experience which I have referred to. At the time I was over in Scotland and at one point while there I slumped into a deep despondency. Everything seemed upsetting and frustrating and foreboding. There had been several acute trials and keen disappointments, and certain persons dear to me, for whose salvation I had prayed for over forty years, were seemingly as alienated from God as ever. It seemed as though the promises of the Bible were like pie crust. Was it any use praying longer? I was having trouble with deafness. And along with that, tinnitus. Loud noises in both my ears day and night incessantly, almost dementing.

A few days after that I had to preach morning and evening at the largest church in that area. And the prospect of it with my ear disability greatly upset me. And a few days after that preaching appointment I had to address ALL the ministers in that area. And the thought of that, with my double ear trouble and other things, almost had me out for the count. Do you know what that means? Out for the count? That's how I felt at the time.

I was nervy, bitterly disappointed, deeply discouraged, and I went to bed weary with mental wrestling and frustration. And then, somewhere between night and morning, September 6th and 7th, something happened that changed everything. I heard no audible voice but someone had wakened me amid the curtains of the night; and was speaking within me. By a language which I knew at once. He said, "Sid! Sid! Are you forgetting Philippians 4: verses 6 and 7? Those verses six and seven perfectly match September six and seven. You've been forgetting the thanksgiving. Hand everything over to Me Sid. And start praying again with

thanksgiving. And start believing that what you ask for
becomes yours. TRY IT Sid. And if you do Philippians
4:6 and 7 is all yours."

Well, I can't explain it too coherently but that is just what
I did. In bed, there and then, amid the nocturnal darkness
I handed everything over to Him. And I started praying
again with thanksgiving. Somehow I did it with ease and
then suddenly Philippians 4:6 and 7 was like an electric
bulb turned on. And I saw everything with illuminating
difference and clearness. My mental tension and gloom had
gone. My anxiety had dropped away like a broken fetter. I
felt renewed and so indeed I was. Soon after, I jumped out
of bed and went downstairs for my time of early-morning
prayer. And it was then that I began to realize something
else. My hearing was better! I could hear everything now
distinctly. And the ear noises had gone—completely. My
whole nervous system had become relaxed. And as I prayed
with thanksgiving—I could never forget it—the peace of
God invaded my heart like a gentle zephyr. Or some halcyon calm. God had put a new song in my mouth—and
I'm still singing it. And I'm singing it here this morning in
Bellevue. You can't hear it but God can! And He can put
a new song in your heart and life. You're needing to learn
all over again the magnificent reality that this text of mine
this morning represents. Dear Christian believer, do you
have this peace in your heart?

The peace that nothing can either destroy or disturb.
Over yonder in California, where my precious wife and I
live, we have a California state lottery. Putting it in healthy
Scottish, "I'm agin it." Once a week a pretty young lady
comes on television to announce the winner of twenty million dollars. I would sooner have this peace of God fill-
ing my heart and mind than I would win twenty million
dollars in the California state lottery. Oh I still have 7/8's
of a minute.

I want to ask you again dear Christian believer. Have
you reached this point of utter surrender? Of all you are and

all you have? You can't buy this peace of God with twenty times twenty million dollars, but you can have it without money or without price if only He gets you altogether. Have you got this peace?[1]

After that, he sat down in the big soft chair next to Adrian Rogers; the congregation stood and applauded. Eyes were wet that morning—including those of J. Sidlow Baxter.

Heaven could have been cheated that day had J. Sidlow Baxter given in to his ill-feeling body and remained in Santa Barbara. Forever faithful and obedient, he not only endured a terrifying plane ride, but he also preached brilliantly while suffering a terrible bout of acid reflux. At an age when most men are content to sit in their rockers, the eighty-eight-year-old Sid preached his heart out that day and never once let the congregation know he was not feeling well. Regarding the aforementioned, of heaven being cheated had he remained in California, Dr. Baxter was unaware that in the audience that morning was a man undecided about his position in Christ. He too suffered from tinnitus. The peace that Dr. Baxter spoke of was something he desired. When the gospel invitation was given at the end of his sermon, this young man went forward to settle his position with Christ. He went on to become an itinerant foreign missionary, building several churches in South America and leading others to Christ. The body of Christ is a wonderful circle of never-ending grace.

||||||||||||||||||||||||||||||||||||||||||||||||||||||||||||||||||||||||||||||||||

THE ITINERANT PREACHING

In journeyings often, in perils of waters, in perils of robbers, in perils by mine own countrymen, in perils by the heathen, in perils in the city, in perils in the wilderness, in perils in the sea, in perils among false brethren; in weariness and painfulness, in watchings often, in hunger and thirst, in fastings often, in cold and nakedness. Beside those things that are without, that which cometh upon me daily, the care of all the churches.

2 CORINTHIANS 11:26–28

The Globe-Trotter

There is a photograph of F. B. Meyer standing at a train station. His venerability is readily apparent as his elderly frame faces the camera. Dressed for travel, he is wearing a black topcoat and hat; one hand holds an umbrella and satchel. His black shoes are polished. What makes the photo unique is this: though his hair is white and his face sagging, a certain boyishness emanates from his countenance. He sports an air of excitement. In his travel satchel is his Bible; he is on his way to a preaching engagement. He looks like he cannot wait to get there.

It is the same thrill that grips the heart of many a retired pastor who embarks on an itinerant preaching ministry. Though they may often feel frail and lacking energy, many an old preacher has felt a rush of blood course through his veins, giving him instant motivation to climb into yet another pulpit. Many great men of faith have entered this kind of journey. W. Graham Scroggie spent years as an itinerant preacher when he left Charlotte Chapel. It made good sense to J. Sidlow Baxter to follow in the sanctified footsteps of others. After all, the apostle Paul never stayed in one place too long.

When J. Sidlow Baxter was a mere boy, he heard F. B. Meyer preach. The saintly Meyer was forever Baxter's hero. Then, when F. B. Meyer was an old man, he heard J. Sidlow Baxter preach. An incident in the life of Meyer sums up why many men who pastor churches seldom remain in a rocking chair upon retirement. He was conducting meetings in western Australia.

"I shall never forget," says Dr. Boreham of Melbourne, "meeting Dr. Meyer on his arrival in this city. I had not seen him since I was a member of his Saturday afternoon Bible Class at Aldersgate Street, thirty years before. I thought I had never beheld such a vision of venerable saintliness as he represented as he stepped from the train. It was at the beginning of July—our Australian mid-winter—and, as it happened, the week that he spent in Melbourne was the wettest, wintriest week that we had known for years. Yet, every afternoon and every evening, the great church was crowded. He looked pitifully frail as he emerged from the vestry and made his way to his seat that he occupied both when resting and speaking. Yet everybody was electrified by the vigour with which he spoke; and, to this day, one often hears of the deep impressions made. Twice during that memorable week, it was my privilege to take tea with him. 'You must get very tired,' I remarked, 'with all this travelling and interviewing and writing and preaching!' 'My dear fellow,' he replied, with his characteristic smile, 'I love it! I love it!' And it was perfectly clear that he did."[1]

From 1955 to 1960 it was clear that J. Sidlow Baxter loved to travel and preach. He and Ethel managed an intense schedule that took them all over the globe. After Ethel's death he continued to travel and preach—leading him to meet Isa in Scotland. Then, he and Isa traveled. He was always in a hurry to get to the next meeting. He was graciously permitted to occupy well-known pulpits among various denominations. Being a Baptist did not keep him from speaking to Methodists, Presbyterians, Congregationalists, Lutherans, Episcopalians, Anglicans, and other Protestant groups.

Sid loved nature. Often, while at a meeting, he would steal away to find a forest or stream where he could contemplate and commune with God's creation. He took delight in a bubbling brook or a bird singing overhead. He frequently used scenes from nature to bring forth a truth from the Gospels or Christian life. He did this to charming effect in a sermon he preached at Bellevue Baptist Church:

> I remember years ago when I was holding meetings in Eugene, Oregon on a lovely, balmy late spring day. I went and sat by the river on a grassy bank just near a very picturesque stone bridge that spanned the river. And as I squatted there I heard a little lapping sound at the edge of the river, and out from the water came a little frog. And I looked at it and

it looked at me and just gave a wink. So I said, "Howdy." And it said, "Howdy." And we just had a nod and a wink and I didn't want to interrupt his morning travels. But I watched. He went from the riverbank along the grass to the great big bridge; and I saw him get to the bridge and stop and look up. So I really thought it was time to have another word with him and I said, "My dear little man you'll never do it. Frogs were never equipped to get over bridges that big. Now you know that don't you? I think you better go back in the water." And being a wise little frog and recognizing my inherent erudition he took my advice and plunked into the water again. But just before he went into the water, both he and I looked up into the sky. We couldn't help it because we heard a gentle swish, swish, swish. And there was a great big, lovely sea gull and the sea gull just looked down at the little frog and winked. And gave a passing glance at me and winked with the other eye, and then just flapped right over the bridge. And I said, "You see little frog, what's an awful problem to you down there is no problem to the gull up there."

Have you got my little parable? Paul says we are not fighting flesh and blood. Don't try and win the battle down here, get up there! The Holy Spirit will give you wings—you'll be on a higher spiritual level. And that higher spiritual level will chasten and cleanse, renew and purify, and empower the mind. And you'll love the Holy. You'll find yourself on a higher level and instead of trying to win by repression you'll be having victory in the Holy Spirit.[2]

Through his preaching at various pulpits around the world, J. Sidlow Baxter took many of his listeners to a higher level.

The Bellevue Meetings

Founded in 1903, Bellevue Baptist Church in Memphis, Tennessee, has a long tradition of pulpit greatness

Dr. Sidlow Baxter and Mrs. Isa Baxter signing autographs

and yielded congregations. Dr. R. G. Lee, the pastor from 1927 to 1959, was so well liked that three biographies were published on his life. Dr. Adrian Rogers, who has been the pastor of Bellevue since 1972, has an international television and radio ministry, Love Worth Finding Ministries. He, too, is much loved by his swelling congregation of thirty thousand.

Adrian and Sid shared a common denominator—their love for Jesus. Each man had achieved an intimacy with Christ that comes only from long hours spent with him. And, as a grain of wheat must first fall to the ground and die before producing a harvest, Adrian Rogers and J. Sidlow Baxter knew what it meant to die to self so that Jesus could produce a rich harvest through them. Their mutual respect for one another made for a fast friendship. Baxter loved coming to Bellevue as much as the people of Bellevue loved having him. He came for a series of meetings in 1977, 1979, 1983, and then lastly in 1991. In 1977, Ethel accompanied him (she died later that same year). From 1979 on, his new bride, Isa, was by his side every time he came to Bellevue.

Each man had a devoted wife. Adrian has Joyce, who has been his companion since their youth. Gifted in her own right as an author, singer, and teacher of women's conferences, Joyce Rogers has been the perfect pastor's wife. She was a gracious hostess to the Baxters and was a great fan of Sid's. In the 1960s, Joyce and Adrian were living in West Palm Beach, Florida, where he pastored a nearby church. After a devastating personal loss, Joyce was browsing in a bookstore when she saw a book entitled, *Going Deeper*, by J. Sidlow Baxter. She began to peruse the pages, and its message touched her heart. It was a time in her life when she was seeking a deeper walk with Jesus; Baxter's theme in the book centered on how to have a deeper walk with him. It was the perfect medicine for her at that critical time.

The members of Bellevue Baptist Church still speak fondly of Baxter, and how he touched their lives. The following is a sermon Baxter preached there on March 1, 1977. It can be ordered through Love Worth Finding Ministries. The message centers on the text in Philippians 3:10: "That I may know him, and the power of his resurrection, and the fellowship of his sufferings, being made conformable unto his death."

It was Sid's favorite Bible verse—he autographed his books with it beneath his signature. The sermon is representative of his preaching style during this time period, but one can listen to it twenty-five years later and still enjoy its timeliness and humor. The message will grip one's heart with its profound teachings and anointed delivery by its humble messenger. Here it is in its entirety:

John chapter eleven, verse five. Jesus in connection with Martha, Mary and Lazarus. And it says this, "Now Jesus loved Martha, and her sister, and Lazarus." It would have

133

been a grammatical economy to say Jesus loved the trio. But our Dear Master is not concerned with mere grammatical economies. Jesus doesn't love us on block or in groups or even in trios or pairs. He loves us with a wonderful, individualizing affection. Just pause and reflect on this. Jesus loves you. And I'm luxuriating again in the thought: Sid, Jesus loves you. I don't think any of us has any suspicion yet how exquisitely tender and individualizing our Dear Savior's love for us is. It was the supreme thrill of the Apostle Paul you know. "The son of God loved us." No. "The son of God loved *me*." And when he thought all he had been—the most violent persecutor of the church—I think he wondered all the more, "The son of God loved me."

Do I need to remind you that Martha and Mary were remarkably opposite in character and traits? Busy, bossy, bustling, managerial Martha. Quiet, reserved, retiring, contemplative Mary. Could you think of two sisters more remarkably different from each other? Now Jesus loved Martha and her sister and Lazarus. Somebody once asked the famous Divine Augustine which of the two he would have preferred, Martha or Mary. And after solid pause the famous Divine replied, with heaven-given strategy, "I think I would sooner have Martha before dinner, and Mary after!"

Yes. Now Jesus loved Martha and her sister and Lazarus. Now Jesus loved Andrew and his brother Simon Peter. What a difference. Rather bashful, retiring Andrew. Impetuous, sometimes stormy, brilliantly eloquent Simon. Now Jesus loved Andrew. Jesus loved Peter. And Jesus loved Matthew. And Jesus loved John, and so it goes, right on to this room and this meal and this meeting. And Jesus loves you.

Why didn't Jesus make you a D. L. Moody or R. A. Torrey or a Wilbur Chapman or a Billy Graham? Or an Adrian Rogers. I'll tell you why. You mean more to Him as you, than you could ever possibly be as someone else. You see, you and I—each of us is unique. Your love can mean to the Dear Wonderful Son of God what mine never can. What no one else's never can. I hope you're listening. And

I hope you're believing this is true. You mean something to the heart of Jesus that no one else in the universe does. And, just because of that, Jesus wants to be to you what He cannot be to anyone else. There's always that wonderful reciprocity about it. You mean something to Him that no one else does. And He therefore wants to be to you what He can't be to anyone else. And if you can receive it, He wants to do something and be something and say something through you that He can't through anyone else. And you mustn't think that because your circumstances may be other than you think they should. Don't think because you may not have the intellectual apparatus that some others do or the financial resources that others have or some social position which is not as high as that of others. Don't you be swept off your feet by any such delusions as that making you less important to Jesus. We're all briefly in school in this present life. There will be no distinction between socially high and socially low in the beyond. There won't even be the distinction between male and female. There will be no distinction between clergy and laity, between the better educated and the lesser educated. No, no, no. Look, I'm speaking with utter sincerity when I say this: again and again when I stand to preach I know of many of those who listened to me—in the beyond will be in a far higher kind of ministry than this poor little man. I'm under no mistake about that. I know Sidlow Baxter better than anybody else in this room. And my conflict is—I come back to it again and again—Sid, Jesus loves you for yourself. Jesus is training you by the Heavenly Paraclete for some dear high ministry he has in the beyond. The troubles and the trials, the sufferings and the adversities which He permits; they are all part of the wonderful tuition doing something in your character preparing you for that wonderful ministry in the beyond. Have no doubt about it. Jesus loves *you*. Just as you are in your basic self.

What is it we sing? "I'm so glad that our Father in Heaven tells of his love in the book He has given. Wonderful things in the Bible I see this is the dearest that Jesus loves us." No. This is the dearest that Jesus loves *me*. Never you be jealous of me and I'll never be jealous of you. You've got Him and I've got Him. We're each special to Him.

Now Martha and her sister and Lazarus—do you know whenever I think of them my mind just jumps on to Philippians chapter 3, verse 10. "That I may know him (Christ) and the power of his resurrection and the fellowship of his suffering." I wonder if you've happened to have noticed the parallel. That I may know Him. That's Martha. And the power of the resurrection. That's Lazarus. And the fellowship of his sufferings. That's Mary.

Now Martha was distinguishably the woman who knew. When our Lord got to Bethany and found that Lazarus had been in the tomb four days, Martha ran out to meet Him. Mary lingered in the house contemplatively—by the way isn't that just like the two sisters? Martha went to meet. Mary remained in the house where she still was. And when Martha accosted our Lord she said, "Lord. If thou hadst been here my brother would not have died." Then she added, "but I know even now whatsoever thou asketh of God He give it." I know—she said. Well, thank God of that. Solid rock amid the swirling waters of her grief. I *know*. Jesus said unto her, "Martha. Thy brother shall rise again." "I know (out it comes again) that he shall rise again at the resurrection in the last day." Jesus said again to Martha, "I am the resurrection and the life. He that believeth on me though he shall have died he shall live again. And whosoever is living and believing on Me shall never die." He shall be translated because our Lord is both the resurrection to the departed and He is the life to those who will be suddenly changed. "Martha believeth thou this." And Martha gave this sublime reply, "I believe that thou art the Christ the Son of God. The savior who should come into the world."

She was right as to His Messianic office: "I believe that thou art the Christ." She was right as to His intrinsic person—the Son of God. And she was right as to His redeeming mission—the Savior who shall come into the world. That's why I say Martha was distinguishably the woman who *knew*. Out it comes three times. I know. I know. I believe!

Now Lazarus was distinguishably the one who knew the power of our Lord's resurrection. We're told seven things about Lazarus. 1. He was dead. 2. He was raised. 3. He was bound. 4. He was loosed. 5. He was feasting (early verses of chapter twelve tell of fellowship). And 6. He was witness bearing. And 7. He was mightily convincing; because by reason of him many of the Jews went their way and believed in Jesus. Got it? 1, 2, 3, 4, 5, 6, 7. Dead, raised, bound, loosed, feasting, witnessing, convincing. He knew the power in *type* of our Lord's resurrection. And he knew in experience the inward reality of being raised.

Mary distinctively was the woman who knew the fellowship of his sufferings. Have you noticed we read of Mary just three times in the Gospels? First, in Luke 10. Second, in John 11. And third, in John 12. In Luke 10 we read, "that while Martha was cumbered about with much serving Mary sat at His feet, to learn His word." Then in John 11, Mary at last comes out of the home and falls at Jesus' feet—pouring out her heart, "Lord." said she, like Martha. "If thou hadst been here!" Third, in John 12, we find that Mary takes an expensive jar of alabaster (some precious perfume from the north of Africa). And she broke that costly alabaster at our Lord's feet. And suddenly the sweet aroma pervaded the whole house so that the guests began to say, "Oh, what a delicious fragrance where is that from?" Have you got it? Those three references to Mary. Luke 10, she sat at His feet to *learn*. John 11, she brought to his feet her *grief*. John chapter 12, she laid at His feet her *best*. A beautiful *type* of consecration. You following? Say yes! Now Jesus loved Martha and her sister and Lazarus and He loves you and He loves me. And the dominating hunger of our Lord's heart is: that because He loves you separately and specially, you will specially seek to know

137

Him and the power of His resurrection and the fellowship of His sufferings.

Pastor. Friends. I want to say to you with love and earnestness, comparatively speaking (and I underline the comparative). Comparatively speaking, there's nothing else worth living for but to get to know Jesus better and better and better.

Christianity was never built on a coffin lid. The skull and crossbones was never our ensign. Mohammad is dead. Buddha is dead. The Hindu sages are dead. But Jesus is *alive!* And His last word was, "Lo, I am with you everyday even to the end!" And it should be the sacred ambition, the over-mastering passion, of our life to get to know Him better and better and better. And He's just waiting. Do you know something? I get very disturbed about this. That when at last, whether we go by the valley of the shadow or amid the shining glory of the second advent, I get disturbed with apprehension lest many of us, when at last we meet Jesus, won't know Him. I didn't say won't recognize Him. Oh, when we see Him amid the unutterable splendors of the heavenly Immanuel's land. When we see Him with the seven-fold diadem of deity upon His royal brow. When we see Him amid that flashing glory compared with which the shining of the cherubim and the seraphim is like the dusk. Of course, we will all instantaneously recognize Him. But recognition is one thing. Heart-to-heart knowing is another. Yes, we'll all recognize Him, but will we all personally, closely know Him? You see, when you and I meet the Lord Jesus, in the sweet by and by, our meeting with Him is meant to be the lovely consummation in which at last, we are seeing face-to-face one who for years we knew heart-to-heart.

You know I'm in my 70s now. I'm only telling you that so you won't mistakenly think I'm in my 90s! And I give you my glad testimony. The older I get the happier I am and the better it becomes. And Jesus is nearer and dearer and clearer until sometimes—I want to be useful while I'm here—but sometimes I get such a lovesickness to see Him. Don't you ever feel like that?

Listen to Charles Wesley, "Oh love Divine how sweet thou art. When shall I find my willing heart all taken up by thee?" And then listen, "I thirst." That's pretty strong. "I faint." That's holy lovesickness. "I thirst, I faint, I die to prove the fullness of redeeming love, the love of Christ to me."

Well now, we should hunger and thirst to know that love already in our experience here. Very well, in my closing word let me become interrogative. What are you doing about it? I never dared to show my face in Memphis and in this great church just to preach. You've got a far better preacher here than I am. But I did pray that the Lord would use my simple way and humble presence to say a word to your hearts in the Savior's name. I want you, the members of this church and visiting friends; I want you to make this mealtime the glad crisis time when you will make the resolve. That from this noonday meal you will become a praying Christian as never before. I've read this and that and the other, biography or autobiography, of great saints. And many of them near their departing for the glory have said, if they had their time to go over again they would pray more. I've yet to read any Christian biography in which the person being recorded ever said, "If I had my time to go over again I wouldn't waste so much time in prayer!" You'll never find *that*.

And if you will give time to seek Him you'll find Him. But mark this. It will have to be a matter of Godly resolve. You will have to say, "I resolve that by thy grace and strength I will be regular in daily quiet withdrawments for prayer to thee." And as soon as you make that resolve, get ready, you'll be the devil's target. If you can lick the devil there, you'll lick him everywhere. But if he beats you there, you'll not really win anywhere. There's no rich experience of Christ apart from constant, daily, unhurried prayer. And oh, we're so slow to learn it, we're always "going to." Like Herod intending after Easter.

Ministers here, I don't care how great a preacher you are. What academic prowess you may have. No minister has a mighty ministry for Christ unless he's a man of prayer. If there's going to be any significant moving of God's Spirit in and over the U.S.A., it will be in answer to prayer. And I believe if only we can get the evangelical minority down to its knees, prosecuting a prayer warfare on behalf of America; I believe that the praying minority could determine the destiny of America. I believe it because God is *still on the throne* and God still hears the prayers of the *few* on behalf of the *many*.

Let's come back to this tomorrow, meanwhile just a word of prayer. And now, Dear Savior, the king of love with nail prints in thy hands and feet. Lift upon us the scepter of thy blessings. Crown us more consciously than ever hitherto with thy loving kindness and tender mercy. Let thy peace possess our hearts. For thy dear name's sake. And may our Father's love and the Savior's grace and all the comforts of the heavenly comforter be in our hearts and in our homes until at last in the Father's house we meet never to part. Amen.[3]

The Canada Meetings

In 1955, J. Sidlow Baxter captured the hearts of Canadian Christians. J. Sidlow Baxter loved the solitude of nature. He enjoyed Canada, from its prairie wheat fields to the Rocky Mountain lakes. Sid delighted in God's creation and his heart thrilled at the beauty of Canada's vastness each time he crossed the Canadian border. He crossed denominational borders as well, for he was warmly welcomed in the pulpits not only of Baptists (his denomination), but also Methodists, Presbyterians, Congregationalists,

J. Sidlow Baxter in Toronto, Canada, in 1988

Lutherans, Episcopalians, Anglicans, Pentecostal, and Christian Alliance churches. Sid loved people and they loved him; he used to pray "Lord, make me winsome so that I may win some!" His messages from the Bible transcended denominational barriers—very few preachers can accomplish that.

His busy schedule in Canada commenced in 1955 and lasted through 1988. The following is his Canadian itinerary, provided by a friend of his in Canada, Mrs. Clara Caddell, who gleaned the information from her husband's diary from 1954 to 1988.

Dr. J. Sidlow Baxter in Canada

December, 1955	Calvary Church, Pape Avenue, Toronto
	Cook's Presbyterian Church, Toronto
March, 1956	CMBC Banquet, Royal York Hotel, Toronto
July, 1956	Bible Hour Speaker, 45th Annual Gideon Convention, Moncton, New Brunswick
July, 1957	Bible Hour Speaker, Canadian National Gideon Convention, Vancouver, British Columbia
August, 1958	Canadian Keswick Conference, Ferndale, Ontario
July, 1961	Gideon Canadian and International Convention, 62nd Anniversary
	Bible Hour Speaker, Royal York Hotel, Toronto
September, 1961	Gideon 3—Millionth Scripture Presentation Banquet, Royal York Hotel, Toronto
October, 1961	The People's Church, Toronto
July, 1967	The People's Church, Toronto

October, 1972	The People's Church, Toronto
April, 1986	The People's Church, Toronto Ontario Bible College and Theological Seminary
	Gideon Banquet, Royal York Hotel, Toronto
	The Chapel of Buffalo, Buffalo, NY
Date uncertain	Philpott Memorial Tabernacle, Hamilton, Ontario
Date uncertain	Jarvis Street Baptist Church, Toronto
Date uncertain	Knox Presbyterian Church, Toronto
May, 1988	The People's Church, Toronto

The following anecdotes from his Canada meetings give a portrait of Baxter as a person. They are graciously provided by Clara Caddell of Toronto.

During the Canadian National Gideon Convention held in Vancouver, B.C. in 1957, Dr. Baxter was the Bible Hour Speaker. The organization's efficient treasurer, anxious to cover all the bases, asked Dr. Baxter if he would submit his expenses for breakfasts, laundry, etc. (Lunches and dinners were already provided.) Dr. Baxter said there were none to submit, for he did his own laundry in the hotel room and had gone to the grocery store and purchased cereal and anything else he required for breakfast, which he prepared for himself. That speaks volumes: he was very prudent in the use of what he considered to be the Lord's money.

At the People's Church, Toronto, as in many other churches, there is always one person who feels it is his, or her, calling to confront every visiting speaker with tough questions usually asked by skeptics. One such person was waiting for Dr. Baxter as he came down from the platform.

143

Sidlow in Canada

Sidlow speaking at a Gideons' meeting in Canada

Dr. Baxter was gracious, patient and courteous. When I remarked about his handling of this "perpetual nuisance," Dr. Baxter said, "If I am not the same off the platform as I am on it, my ministry is worthless."

When Dr. Baxter was to speak (which was for the last time) at The People's Church in Toronto, Canada, he phoned us from Santa Barbara to ask if I would get some things for him and put them in the hotel room refrigerator. Dr. Baxter was diabetic and had to be careful about his diet (not only that, but he was a private person and kept things like physical limitations close to his chest). He wanted fruit and, of course, a teapot and tea. When we took him to his hotel, he saw his beautiful room, equipped with a study desk and other comforts, and he saw the well-stocked frig, he went over to the bed, fell on his knees, and thanked the Lord for His goodness. That's the kind of man Dr. Baxter was.

To my husband, Wilbur Caddell, and me, J. Sidlow Baxter was a true, kind and precious friend, spiritual advisor, mentor, gifted, devoted and ever gracious minister of God's Word. Knowing him and his dear wife Isa has been one of the richest blessings of God in our lives. We phoned one another often and most times those calls ended with prayer and Sid saying, "In your walk, may the Lord be nearer and clearer and dearer than He has ever been before."

It was in Canada that Reverend Baxter became Dr. Baxter. Mariana Coldwell, the alumni secretary of Heritage College and Seminary (formerly Central Baptist Seminary) provided the following speech, given by Dr. W. G. Brown, dean of the seminary, in 1956.

Born in Australia of a Godly mother, J. Sidlow Baxter was converted in his teens. His early education he received in St. James' School, in the town of Ashton-under-Lyne, Lancashire, England, and then in the School of Technology in the same place. His spare time he used to study music. This useful attainment for a "brief but happy period" he specially used when he travelled as pianist to the National Young Life Campaign. He became a preacher as a boy and a popular one.

For four years he studied theology at Spurgeon's College, London, and then went to the pastorate. From 1928 to 1932 he was in Northampton, 1932–1935 at the noted Bethesda Chapel, Sunderland. Then he answered a second call to what, according to "The Life of Faith", is perhaps the most distinctly evangelical of the many churches in Scotland's capital, Charlotte Baptist Chapel. His predecessors were famous, including Joseph W. Kemp, and W. Graham Scroggie, and the congregation numbered about a thousand. Here under Pastor Baxter hundreds were converted and many led into full time service. For months at a time Edinburgh's largest hall was used with Sunday evening services of two to three thousand. A preacher he was, and a strong one, but equally a real teacher of the word "with his own approach and method", whose weekly Bible Classes attracted many.

Increasingly he was drawn to convention and conference work. Audiences in London, England, and Ocean Grove, America, reached twelve thousand at one time. He was also

146

popular in his native land of Australia and on many mission fields. A world itinerary, begun a year ago January, but preceded by six lecture tours in America and Canada, has carried him far. Through his printed message, and especially his unique volumes, *Explore the Book*, he has covered the whole Bible, reaching many.

Mr. President, in honour of his eminent Christian character, his thorough knowledge of and faithfulness to the Holy Scriptures, and his outstanding service to the cause of Christ, I ask you confer on him the degree of Doctor of Divinity of Central Baptist Seminary, honoris causa.

The Canadians who heard Dr. Baxter during those many tours still speak fondly of him; their testimony speaks loudly of his fidelity as an international preacher of the Word of God.

The University Baptist Church Meetings

In the picturesque setting of the northwestern Arkansas hills lies the quiet college town of Fayetteville. Apart from the rustle of falling leaves, the idyllic calm is otherwise disturbed only when the University of Arkansas fans "call the hogs" with their cries of, "Woooooooooo, Pig! Sooie!" that bellow forth from the Donald W. Reynolds Razorback Stadium.

The chaplain of the Razorback team is H. D. McCarty, an affable man who commands respect from the athletes. He is also a brigadier general in the Air National Guard. He has also been the pastor of University Baptist Church since 1965. During that long pastorate he has ministered to some twenty thousand students, hosted a regional television and radio ministry, and has grown the church's mission budget from $5,000 annually in 1965 to an annual investment of over $350,000. He is also the reason why a certain

BONNYHAME
914 SKY VIEW DRIVE
SANTA BARBARA
CALIFORNIA 93108

Mr F. Tanner Riley,   25th. July, 1986.
104, Willow Oak Court,
Starkville, Miss. 39759.

Dear Tanner,

How pleased we were to receive your letter yesterday, and how
kind of you to write. Thank you. We are grateful to know that you are now
comfortably and happily settled in your new home and your new ministry. We
hope you and your dear Thelma will have rewarding fulfilments and continuing
blessing through all your years there. That will be the emphasis in all our
prayers for you. I have just been looking up on the map to find exactly the
whereabouts of Starkville. There doesn't seem anything "stark" about it. I
should think it is a very pleasant place, even though maybe a bit hot in the
summer. And what you say about the musical ministry at the church, and its
pastor, along with the new Baldwin and Yamaha grand pianos, is all exceedingly
interesting. In sheer rivalry (would you believe it!) this morning there is
to be delivered here a new Steinway baby grand which we have purchased. At
our time of life we are glad it is the only "baby" we shall have around, with
a different kind of music! What you tell us about your new choir is particularly interesting, Tanner. May you and they blend in ever-increasing useful
service and esteem for each other.

Isa and I want to be specially remembered to Thelma. We sympathetically
enter into what you tell us about her --especially relating to her mother and
father in their present trials. Even as I write we are praying for her and for
them. Thank you for up-dating us about the Riley family. They, too, are under
our prayer umbrella. What to say in reply to your kind suggestion about the
possibility of our visiting your new church sometime, I scarcely know. I am
not doing much these days by way of "travel" ministry. I am spending more time
writing and trying to get a long-delayed tape ministry going. Certainly, if we
are ever anywhere reasonably near to Starkville we will jump at the chance to
come and visit with you. We shall always thank God that we came to know you
at Fayetteville. We know also how keenly the dear folk there miss you now that
you are no longer there. Yes, Tanner, we shall keep praying for Fayetteville.
I must not add more. We are just preparing to leave for New Jersey --and shall
be over there one week. GOD GREATLY BLESS YOU.

Over with our love & esteem
Sid

Englishman came to love the little town of Fayetteville and
the people there.

Perhaps the quaintness of Fayetteville gladdened the
heart of J. Sidlow Baxter and reminded him of those long-
ago Pennine Hills of Lancashire, England. But one thing

148

BONNYHAME
914 SKY VIEW DRIVE
SANTA BARBARA
CALIFORNIA 93108

12th. December, 1985.

Mr F. Tanner Riley,
University Baptist Church,
Fayetteville, Arkansas 72701.

My treasured friend,

By the time this reaches you Isa and I will be in
Australia, where I am to give the morning Bible studies at the Belgrave
Heights Convention (near Melbourne); then several days at Adelaide, and
a final rally at Sydney. If you devote an earnest moment in your prayer-
times, please ask for me a powerful enduing by the Holy Spirit. They will
be large gatherings, and I do not want just to "preach" (you understand).
Thank you, Tanner, for your letter of some days ago, and the choruses enclosed. The latter are beautiful.

I am sending you herewith a bound manuscript containing many of the
J.S.B. hymns and some of my tunes. This bound copy is not the hymnbook
I have told you about, but only my own hymns and tunes. You will recall
my saying that I would send you a few hymns which perhaps you could get
your choir to sing. Here are about a dozen, which are not set to J.S.B.
tunes, but to well-known tunes. I hope you will like the words, and that
you will think they hook on well to the tunes. I have given them in the
order of the at-present usefulness to me. There is no hurry, Tanner. You
can get them sung just when your busy schedule permits. I would stress
the follwing two points. (1) They need to be taped or cassetted on best
quality tape which will truly absorb both the higher and lower reaches of
the music. (2) All expense incurred in purchasing tape or xeroxing the
words will be gladly covered by myself. If you wish, I will gladly send
a sum in advance; or you can let me know as you proceed.

In a few days (or soon after we are back from Australia) I will be
sending you a couple of J.S.B. compositions --both words and music--which
possibly your choir could sing as a kind of mini-anthem some Sunday. They
are a couple which I thought might be a part of a further cantata (if I
can get time!).   My dear Isa unites with me in every warm good wish for
Christmas and all of 1986.

Always cordially in the Name we love,

Cid

J. Sidlow Baxter

is sure: he and H. D. McCarty became like father and
son. Their relationship deepened over the many visits Dr.
Baxter made to Fayetteville from 1974 to 1991. Dr. Baxter
dedicated his book *The Other Side of Death* to McCarty.
In all, J. Sidlow Baxter stood at the pulpit at University

Above top: J. Sidlow Baxter Library, Fayetteville, Arkansas; **above bottom:** J. Sidlow Baxter's desk chair, and typewriter; **opposite top:** portrait of J. Sidlow Baxter in the library; **opposite bottom:** main room of the library.

Baptist Church an incredible fifty-six times. There are only three other places where he preached more frequently: Northampton, Sunderland, and Edinburgh—all his own pastorates. H. D. McCarty and his wife, Shirley, entertained the Baxters (first Sid and Ethel, later Sid and Isa) each time; a warm friendship ensued.

151

This is why the J. Sidlow Baxter Library exists in the little town of Fayetteville. It is here in "The Treasure Room" one can see Dr. Baxter's personal belongings, such as his private library, desk, chair, and typewriter. For the past twenty years the library has expanded steadily under the direction of Ruth Ann Stites. The collection boasts more than seventeen thousand volumes, which serve the needs of Ouachita Baptist University, the University Baptist Church congregation, as well as the student body of the University of Arkansas. For the J. Sidlow Baxter fan, it is a supreme thrill to hold a tattered copy of *The Pulpit Commentary* (his favorite commentary) while sitting in his chair at the desk where he wrote so many of his wonderful books.

A portrait of Dr. Baxter in the main room stares down at the students who busily study in the library that bears his name. His vast hymn collection is maintained there as well. A lover of the "old-time hymns," Dr. Baxter composed several hundred hymns. He even had some of them (as well as a cantata) performed at University Baptist Church under the direction of F. Tanner Riley, retired minister of music. In fact, it was Tanner Riley's love for the old hymns that struck a fond chord in the musical heart of J. Sidlow Baxter. Through this common denominator, Dr. Baxter and Tanner Riley became close friends.

The congregation and staff at University Baptist Church remember J. Sidlow Baxter fondly. In fact, McCarty will not let them forget the man who was like a father to him; he speaks his name continually and performs an excellent impersonation of Sid. McCarty performed the funeral service for his beloved mentor in Santa Barbara and he helps keep the memory of Dr. Baxter alive. The following is a sermon that J. Sidlow Baxter preached at University Baptist Church; it is representative of his style at the time.

An Octogenarian Testimony

My dear friends, what a pleasant experience it is to be back again at University Baptist Church in Fayetteville. To see so many of yourselves again whom I have had the pleasure of meeting on former visits. And of course, it puts the cream on the milk to renew fellowship with your indefatigable, gifted, beloved pastor and his precious wife. And then of course, it is such a joy to meet again your friend and my esteemed friend Mr. Tanner Riley. And to see and hear again that deft-fingered master of the keyboard, Saint Carol. Mrs. Baxter and I looked forward with peculiarly happy feelings to seeing you all again and to spending these few days with you at our Savior's feet and around His precious Word. I see on the pulpit here there is a metal disk on which there are chiseled the words, "Sir, we would like to see Sidlow." I beg your pardon. It says here, John 12 verse 21, "Sir, we would like to see Jesus." And it is my prayer that this morning, this evening, Monday, Tuesday, Wednesday, Thursday, that is just what will happen—that we shall see Him. And not a mere man. Don't you feel the same? Yes.

Now, I had a shock when I looked at you this morning, not because you are physiognomically peculiar. But your dear pastor—in chatting with me last night at dinner—told me that in the early service we would have the middle-aged and the elderly. And here on the front rows and scattered round the church I see a crowd of wicked-looking young Philistines. Now dear younger friends, I want you to be patient here this morning. All who have heard me minister on former visits know that I seldom use notes. But I am going to use notes this morning if you don't mind, and also you may think that my message in this first service is not peculiarly adapted to you. Now cheer up, there's worse to come. No. If I were giving a title to my message this morning it would have to be, *AN OCTOGENARIAN TESTIMONY*. I heard someone say, "Wow!" Yes that's it. Now let me put my spectacles on. Something I seldom do and I don't really need them, but I want to be careful, you

see I've got to get through by a certain time, because we have another service.

Now are you ready for the ordeal? This morning I am in a retrospective mood and when I tell you why perhaps you will be inclined to forgive me. I have just celebrated my eightieth birthday. Yes. I am now among the prestigious sect of the octogenarians. It seems scarcely credible to me; when I was in my 40s I had reason to doubt whether I would ever survive my 50s. Yet here I am in my 80s feeling younger and better than in my 40s. Maybe it is almost inevitable that as we grow elderly we grow reminiscent. We have so much more to look back on than when we were in our youth. Dear youngites here this morning, if you knew how sorry I am for you, you'd get up and stay here. Aristotle called memory, the scribe of the soul. The older we grow the more does that busy scribe write on the parchment of our minds. And often, he gets us older folks talking about our past until we become a perfect nuisance to the younger folk. That famous preacher, Charles Haddon Spurgeon, has a pithy comment about elderly ministers who are forever telling anecdotes. Anecdotes about

their past. They tell so many such anecdotes says Spurgeon, that although they have not yet reached their dotage they certainly have reached their anecdote age. So I must be on guard against that naughty snare.

Let me not tax you this morning by being too reminiscent, and yet I do want to give my testimony as a Christian octogenarian. Now, please believe that whatever reference I may make to Sidlow Baxter, it will be intended to point you beyond unworthy little me, to that wonderful Savior who is our dearest treasure. And as a scriptural basis for my testimony this morning, let me appropriate a well-known paragraph in the Psalms. I refer to Psalm 103, verses 1–5. Are you listening?

"Bless Jehovah oh my soul and all that is within me, bless his holy name. Bless Jehovah oh my soul and forget not all his benefits. Who forgiveth all thine iniquities. Who healeth all thine diseases. Who redeemeth thy life from destruction. Who crowneth thee with loving kindness and tender mercies. Who satisfieth thy mouth with good things so that thy youth is renewed like the eagles."

155

That heavenward encomium is a royal soliloquy. For David is addressing himself. Bless Jehovah oh my soul. As the mind is the part that thinks. And as the heart is the part that feels. So the soul is the basic self-aware human person. David wants his whole being to extol his divine benefactor. So he adds, "and *all* that is within me bless his holy name." David knew nothing of psychology in our modern sense but he did know intuitively the complexity of man's inner being. And like the conductor of some grand symphony, he would fain call the whole orchestra into united praise. In fact, I don't know whether you've noticed, but by the time David reaches the end of this Psalm he is calling on all earth and heaven and the universe to join in concert with him. "Bless Jehovah," he says, "Call ye his angels that excell in strength, bless Jehovah all ye hosts that do his pleasure. Bless Jehovah all his works in places of his dominion."

Yes. Sun, moon, and stars. Flaming seraphs, sinless angels, all created intelligences in their myriads. David ambitiously requisitions for his magnificent oratorial. But in the last verse of the Psalm he comes right back again to this: "And bless Jehovah oh my soul." Brothers and sisters in our holy calling, how good it is to feel like that toward our faithful Creator Father. Not only does it honor God, it has a reflex effect upon ourselves. To be habitually praiseful to God is one of the best therapies for our nervous system. And a definite contributor to our health in general. If you want to keep thoroughly fit and well, keep full of the joy of gratitude to God.

So now, let us look more particularly at this opening paragraph. As soon as David has said, "forget not all his benefits," he lists five of the greatest. First he says, "Who forgiveth all thine iniquities." That comes first of course because it is our first need. We're sinners. There can be no fellowship with God until we are forgiven. And *oh* what a price Almighty God paid that you and I might have a blood bought, whole and free, and final forgiveness for sin. For the honour of His own Holy Name and for the safety of

His big family, the universe, God's Holiness necessitated that atonement be made for human sin. But what God's Holiness demanded, God's love provided. On Calvary the Divine Holiness and the Divine Love blended in the biggest deed that even God ever did. Of course, the forgiveness of sins and the fellowship with God mean little to the man of the world; the earthly man who lives for the flesh and then drops at death into postmortem darkness and damnation. But to the soul alarmed by the prospect of final judgment, and aroused to the need of getting right with God, to such the blood of Calvary and the forgiveness of God mean everything.

My own conversion to Christ occurred when I was sixteen. Are you listening young folks? Sixteen. For weeks beforehand I had been so convicted and so haunted by my own sinful condition in the sight of God, I was like John Bunyan's fugitive from the city of destruction. You know how John Bunyan tells us that unhappy fugitive found himself lunging about in the slough of despond. Have you read Bunyan's *Pilgrim's Progress* recently? I always have to think carefully before I say that because I heard a preacher not long since speak about John Pilgrim's Bunyan's Progress. Have you read John Bunyan's *Pilgrim's Progress* lately? Well, this escapee from the city of destruction, with a big heavy burden on his back, went wallowing into the slough of despond. However, somehow eventually he struggled out and eventually got to the wicked gate. And so did I also, by the mercy of God, get out of the slough of despond and I got to that wicked gate. Wicked gate, which is the gospel promise, "Believe on the Lord Jesus Christ and thou shalt be saved." At that wicked gate I stood before a cross whereon One hung and bore my sin and died for me. And can I ever forget it—suddenly, as I gazed on Him my own big, heavy guilt burden suddenly snapped from my back and rolled away. And like John Bunyan's pilgrim, I gave three leaps for joy and went on my way rejoicing. And since that happy day which fixed my choice, I have been on the way that leads to the heavenly Zion. I've been daily singing, "Bless Jehovah, oh my soul. Who forgiveth all thine iniquities!"

But now look at David's next strophe, "Who healeth all thine diseases." Now if those words are to be taken in their most obvious sense, they refer not only to spiritual healing, but to healing of the body. They're the words of a man now elderly looking back over the years and thanking God both for special healings and for still vigorous physical health. I feel equally grateful as David this morning. I was hearing of a couple over yonder in England's green and pleasant land. They were octogenarians and they were celebrating their wedding day. And they went to a lovely little town in the country of Cheshire to celebrate it and to reminisce and to tell each other again how much they were in love with each other. But the time went by quickly and it was time to run back and get the railway train home to Manchester. And the dear old husband said, "Come on darling. It is time we were going for the train. We're going to miss it." But she was very sentimental and she said, "Oh Horace isn't this wonderful! Do you know although I've got winter in my hair, I've still got summer in my heart." "Yes darling, I know. But just now I'm wishing you had a bit more spring in your feet!"

Well, I'm glad to report I've never felt better in all my life. I've still got my faculties and plenty spring in my feet—I believe I could race some of you rascals!

Now David had known serious sickness, as some of his Psalms show. For instance, Psalm thirty-eight. "My loins are filled with a loathsome disease and there is no soundness in my flesh." But David had also experienced supernatural healing. See Psalm thirty. "Oh Jehovah my God I cried unto thee and thou hast healed me." Yes. And what thanksgiving now wells up in David's heart as he reviews it all. And how realistically I can associate my own experience with his for I also have known similar healings. May I with lowly gratitude and your permission, may I refer to just one occasion?

In 1965 when I was 63 I had brought upon myself acute diabetes. A crisis developed—I was rushed to hospital. Later we learned I had reached the line beyond which there would have been coma and death. I can hardly describe the desolation that floored me. The whole facade of my cherished plans collapsed. Any further travel ministry preaching the Word seemed a forlorn hope. The sense of bleak frustration just crumpled me. And yet it was just then and there that my Heavenly Master most signally revealed Himself as the one who healeth all thy diseases. I had always been skeptical about those people who claimed to have visions. Constitutionally, I had not of their type.

But, in the hospital, this is what happened: either the second or third morning, when I was emerging from sleep into that hazy semi-consciousness which often precedes full wakefulness—I had a vision. There was a bright amber background, then in the forefront a large print Bible open at this Psalm. Psalm 103. Next, a hand appeared with its index finger pointing to verse 3, "Who forgiveth all thine iniquities." The words shone, they fairly shone with such meaning to me as I can hardly describe to you. They were like a glistening rainbow overarching the whole of my life. What did it basically matter whether I lived or died. Whether I was well or ill. Whether I was this or that. So long as I was eternally saved. Washed in the Blood of the Lamb. Born of the Heavenly Spirit. Forgiven all my trespasses, my guilt forever more obliterated. *Oh thank God!* I saw things in their true perspective. "Who forgiveth all thine iniquities."

The next morning, just at the same time, there it was again. The same vision, only now the index hand moved to the next clause, "Who healeth all thy diseases." The words stood out with a kind of neon glow. Oh, I can see them yet in my mind. They were before my eyes like a neon sign all the rest of that day. I knew as definitely as if a voice had shouted from heaven. "Sid! God is going to heal you." I knew it. The third morning there it was again, the same amber background, the same big open Bible, the same place,

159

Psalm 103. But now the finger had moved again and it was pointing to the next statement, "Thy youth is renewed like the eagle's." I not only saw the words I inwardly felt them. And I grasped that God was not only going to heal me but to so renew me that I would have better health than ever before. Something else flashed into my mind. I had recently been reading about the Grand Climacteric. Do you know what the Grand Climacteric is? Well you've all got a dictionary at home. You'll find it in any normal-sized dictionary. Let me quote my own dictionary—it's an American dictionary. "The Grand Climacteric is the 63rd year, supposed to be a critical year for men." Are you listening men? How old are you? We men have our crises. I won't call it the men-o-pause. But uh yes, there's a constitutional, basically nervous crisis very common in the male in his 63rd year. And there was I in my 63rd year. It was my Grand Climacteric. And God was meeting me in a strangely eye-opening way with forgiving love and healing power and physical health renewal.

He had laid me low to humble me. To teach me more complete dependence on Himself. More prayerful yielded-ness to Him so that He might lift me up reconditioned for service. And soon the signs of healing appeared. My blood sugar level so plummeted that the two excellent doctors who attended me began to wonder whether it was diabetes at all. Or whether it was only a temporary pancreatitis which had brought me to the hospital. Nonetheless, when I left the hospital I was supplied with diet charts and insulin gadgets and a booklet of instructions. Deep down I knew they would never be needed, and they never were. The Lord told me He wanted me to do another ten years of travel ministry. And during those ten years we traveled and preached and lectured and wrote books and put more time in than ever and had more tokens of blessing than ever before. I used to marvel at the energy I had. The simile about mounting up with wings as eagles, from Isaiah, kept coming to my mind. It is now close on twenty years since that illness, and my health has been better and better and better ever since.

Excuse me, *hallelujah*! What lies ahead health-wise I do not know. Divine healing does not make us immortal. Nor does it give us immunity from the Natural Law of cause and effect. I thank God for all medical and surgical skill. I certainly do. And yet I know that above and beyond all that is the *great* Heavenly healer who healeth *all* thy diseases. He does not always heal by supernatural intervening. Where healing can come through natural means God more often uses them. And sometimes too—are you listening elderly-ites?—sometimes too God may allow sickness to linger, in order to teach us lessons which we would not apparently learn in any other way. I know that, looking back, I have learned far more from my times of adversity than I ever learned from my golden days of prosperity. However, there is coming a time when all born again Christian believers will sing in their resurrection bodies, bodies of diseaseless, tireless, immortality. We shall sing, "He has healed all our diseases forever and ever and ever." Is my testimony weary-ing you? Say no. We're getting through very well—really aren't you glad I'm not ninety!

But look now at what comes next in David's peal of praises. He says, "Who redeemeth thy life from destruc-tion." David does not here use that word redeemeth in its theological or New Testament sense, as meaning re-demption from sin. No. David lived a thousand years B.C. remember? And he knew nothing as we now know about the eternal redemption purchase for us on Calvary. David is referring to physical deliverances. It would be nearer the sense of the Hebrew wording if rendered, "Who keeps redeeming thy life from the grave." God knows how to keep His elect alive until their work on earth is done. In the midst of threats and perils, George Whitefield, the eloquent contemporary of John Wesley, said, "I am immortal till my work is done." You can say the same. I can say the same. The Almighty enwraps His elect in the guardian wings of His protective omnipotence. The arrow of death cannot strike you or me until God calls you and me to our

heavenly inheritance. My, what peace of mind that gives!
What courage it gives. None can touch me or you unless
God decides yes. Although I am the unworthiest of our
Master's servants I too can report special providences which
have redeemed my life from the grave.

At least four times I ought to have been dead. I won't tell
you about the four but shall I annoy you if I give you just
one instance? I was being motored up north to give three
monthly lectures at a theological college. We came to a blind
bend in the road, my driver frantically swung the car around
to avoid colliding with some heavy wooden pilings. But in
doing so he crashed through the guard rails on the other
side of the road so that our car hurtled into space twenty-
five feet above a grassy hollow and then it landed on a fairly
steep slope besides a narrow river. In that split second when
we shot into the vacuum above the stream, I knew by swift
telegramatic inward communication, "Sid don't be afraid.
You're not to be killed. You'll not even be hurt. Underneath
you Sid are the everlasting arms." The car was a twisted total
wreck. My driver friend considerably hurt. But I myself did
not have a bruise. I learned later that seven persons had been
killed at that same spot and others maimed for life. In fact,
soon after our accident, the road itself was altered so that it
should be no longer a death trap.

Now doubtless some of you whom I now address could
testify to similarly unmistakable experiences of God's love-
grip upon you in what might have been fatal emergencies.
But best of all there is coming a golden morning when all
of us who are washed in the blood of the Lamb will sing
an amplified version of David's words, "Who redeemeth
thy life from the grave." We shall sing, "He has redeemed
us eternally not only from the guilt and the penalties of
sin. He has redeemed us forever from the dark power of
the grave."

And now see what comes next in David's catalogue of
(wait a minute are you really enjoying this? Let me look
at you. I'll promise I won't use notes again. But you see if

I hadn't used notes this morning we would never get out), see now what comes next in David's catalogue of Jehovah's benefits toward him. Oh isn't this lovely? "Who crowneth thee with loving kindness and tender mercies."

In the early 1900s when I was a little English boy the British Empire was at its maximum. The most far-flung empire in history. Our annual observance of Empire Day, when the bands played and the guns boomed salutes—it was an exciting holiday for us. The crown on our British sovereign's head was the greatest and securest on earth. And yet it was then I learned the old proverb, "Uneasy lies the head that wears the crown." And how true that is of earthly crowns. What tragedies to hundreds of earth's crowned heads. During our twentieth century how suddenly most of Europe's crowns have fallen. But brethren and friends here is an untarnishable crown that never causes its wearer one heartache or one headache. He crowneth thee with loving kindness and tender mercies. Oh what an unspeakable benefit it is to go through life with that daily coronation of loving kindness and tender mercies as a conscious reality. Is it a conscious reality to you? It is meant to be. What royalty and dignity it gives to our life. And what richness and guarantee and gladness.

Look carefully at the wording. Not just kindness, but *loving kindness*. Once, when I was a young man in college, I had a brief illness. I still recall the kindness shown to me by the staff and the students. Soon afterwards, we all went home for the Christmas holidays. And there was my precious mother. And what a welcome she gave me. Oh she showed me kindness, but somehow mother's *kindness* wasn't just like the kindness of the fellows at college. Theirs was kindness, but my precious mother's was *loving kindness*. Such is the father-like, mother-like kindness in the warm bosom of God to you and me. Jesus and Calvary are the proof of it.

And there is a difference also between mercies and tender mercies. Sometimes in a law court a judge will say to a guilty culprit, "You are found guilty but as this is your first offence the court will exercise leniency, and dismiss you with a warning." Well, certainly that is mercy, but you would scarcely call it tender mercy. If you would know what tender mercies are, you must visit that home where a big-hearted weeping, forgiving father is welcoming back his now-repented prodigal boy. You must see the fond embrace, the tears, the kiss, the reassurance that all is forgiven and forgotten. That is no mere law court mercy; that is *tender mercy*. And all God's promises in the Word are the expressions of His tender-hearted mercy to us. What a dear wonderful Jehovah He is!

And that brings us to the last of David's five couplets, "Who satisfieth thy mouth with good things so that thy youth is renewed like the eagle's." Well that's how it reads in our King James version. But there is need for an improved translation here. Leave out that word "mouth"—it is an interloper. It is wrong. The New American Standard Bible seems closest to the Hebrew wording here. And the translation is, "Who satisfies thy years with good things." And which years were those? They were David's elderly years. Yes. That is what he was meaning. He satisfieth thy elderliness. What a sympathetic benefit that is.

When I grasped that such was the meaning of the Hebrew, my heart broke into singing, "Thank you oh Lord for such a consolation to octogenarians. 'Who satisfieth thy elderliness.'" He certainly does satisfy the special needs of the elderly and aged among the generation of His people. I can certainly testify that in my own experience He satisfies my heart now with more goodness than ever. Somehow God and Jesus and the Holy Spirit—to me today—they're nearer and dearer and clearer than ever. I have a joy I never used to have.

You young things here this morning, I'm telling you if you live your life with the Lord Jesus, as you get older you'll have joys compared with which the joys of life's springtime don't compare. Springtime doesn't compare with Autumn when you've lived your life with Jesus. Were you listening to that? Say yes. Yes. If I may say so reverently, old age is

164

thrilling! I know all about your arthritis and your rheumatism and so on. But aren't there some of you agreeing with me? Old age is thrilling when you live it arm-in-arm with Jehovah, the God who walked and talked with Enoch.

What shall we say about that climatic line, "Thy youth is renewed like the eagles"? Does it seem rather overdrawn to liken the aging saint to that majestic bird? Maybe. But I think David had his good reasons. The eagle is not only the king of birds, the largest, strongest, remotest among the creatures of the sky, with pinions outclassing all others. The eagle is a remarkably long-lived bird—did you know that? But even that is not all. Besides the annual molting the eagle is unique in this: that when it is nearly 100 years old it casts all its feathers from its head to its talons. And it has a complete refeathering when it is nearly a hundred years old. That of course is why David uses it for his comparison, "Thy youth is renewed like the eagle's."

How then are we to take David's simile of the eagle? Is it mere hyperbole or poetic elasticity? Possibly. And pardonably so. Yet although not meant to be taken quite literally, it has indeed a realistic parallel with what often happens to the Lord's older folk in the household of the faith. I am now one of them and I know at least a little about it. During the past fifteen years, despite bereavement and nervous strain and continually vexatious pressures, I have known such mental and physical renewing that I can well enter into David's words, "Thy youth is renewed like the eagle's."

Such renewal does not happen to all aging believers, but it does happen to many. One reason is that as we grow older and get a bit wiser and feel a bit weaker, we sense more acutely our need for dependence on God. Therefore we pray more. And find ourselves singing with Isaiah, "They that wait on Jehovah shall renew their strength, they shall mount up with wings of eagles." We find that our prayer times are not just a matter of necessity or duty or privilege or even delight. We find that when we pray we've got to know the Savior so intimately, we're *absorbing! Absorbing! Absorbing!* And we begin to understand the meaning of Paul's words, that the life of the Lord Jesus might be manifest in our mortal bodies. We've all got to die, but I don't think we're all meant to die sick. I think the Lord wants to do something more for us physically, mentally.

I got rather tired of being told, "Sid when you get older your memory will fail you and you won't take things in as quickly." I find the opposite. I've never felt more alert! I never felt that my memory was betraying me. You know the little boy who said (when he was asked what is memory) he said, "Oh memory is the thing you forget with." And I'm told as I get older I shall keep forgetting and forgetting. Don't you think it! You needn't be afraid of getting old if you get to know the Lord. I believe you'll find that in your prayer times with Him you'll be absorbing Him. Absorbing Him. Absorbing Him. And you'll find yourself saying, "Yes, I'm mounting up with wings as eagles."

Oh now that's about it. Are we in time? I don't think we are but can't do anything about it. Let my last word be this; even the eagle, despite its centennial refeathering, eventually dies. But when we Christian seniors discard this mortal flesh we shall be at once in that fair realm where no one is ever tired. Where there are no undertakers and no funerals. No cripples, no infirm, no bedridden. No blind or deaf or dumb. No need for hospitals and no need for eventide homes for the aging. And there, in Emmanuel's land, we shall experience a renewal far more wonderful than the temporary renewal of the eagle. It will be renewal into immortal youth and bloom in the land where the roses never fade and the sun never sets and the night never comes. And disease never invades and death never divides. And where we never say, "Goodbye." We're going to mount up with wings higher than any eagle of the skies ever mounted.

In closing, let me say to the elderly believers, have no fear that God may forget you or overlook you as old age creeps on. No. He will come closer than ever to your inmost consciousness—if you lean more fully on His faithfulness. In a way which younger people can't understand, He will satisfy your deepest need even when you feel externally unwanted. And when outward circumstances are much less than comfortable, He will never fail you, never let you down, never give you up, and never let you go. And to the younger folks here I would say don't be afraid of growing old. It's a wonderful experience to grow old. A wonderfully educative experience. I wouldn't have missed getting old for anything. I've been thrilled by it.

> Pray hear me now that I am eighty
> I give you counsel wise and weighty;
> Unsaved one lest you be too late
> Make haste to yonder wicked gate.
>
> See there the one who bore your sin
> He beckons and invites you in;
> Oh let me help you understand
> That in his tender nail-pierced hand;
> God offers pardon full and free
> And safe forever you shall be.
>
> With guilt removed and sins forgiven
> You'll be a pilgrim bound for heaven;
> Receive that Savior I implore
> Be saved, be saved, forever more.

Dear Harvey, hadn't I better just dismiss with prayer? Now if *you* start we'll be late! And now, may the love of God our Father in Heaven and the grace of His dear Son our precious Savior, and the fellowship of the heavenly Holy Spirit be with all of us till we meet again. Amen. Amen.[4]

eleven

|||||||||||||||||||||||||||||||||||||||||||||||||||||||||||||||||||||||||||||||

THE AUTHOR
AND POET

Study to shew thyself approved unto God, a workman that needeth not to be ashamed, rightly dividing the word of truth.

2 TIMOTHY 2:15

His Masterpiece

There is a room in the Baxter home in Santa Barbara that is aptly called "the blue room." Lovingly decorated by Sid for his dear Isa (whose favorite color is blue), it is the room in the house where they relaxed and enjoyed the evenings. There is a stained glass window above the mantel, which sets off the room (Sid put this window in for Isa), and beside the mantle is a bookcase handmade by Sid. Upon the top shelf lay six blue volumes of Dr. Baxter's magnum opus, *Explore the Book*.

Originally given as a series of Bible lectures on Thursday evenings at Charlotte Chapel in Edinburgh, *Explore the*

Book is a masterwork. How can one explore its voluminous pages without experiencing a feeling of awe? Since its publication in 1960, thousands of pastors and Sunday school teachers have turned to its informative chapters over and over again. Dr. Adrian Rogers has said of *Explore the Book* (he has often referred to it as his next favorite book beside the Bible), "if you will read it and answer the questions at the end of each chapter you will have the equivalent of a seminary education."[1]

Explore the Book is not your average Bible commentary. Because of its author's singular uniqueness, it reads like a great literary work. And, because of its conversational style, both pastor and layperson can appreciate its profound applications. Continuously in print for over forty years, it has stood the test of time. Since 1966 it has been bound in one large volume. Dr. John Phillips, who in turn is well known for his commentary series, *Exploring the Bible*, stated in regard to helping a certain Bible student build a strong library for personal use, "*Explore the Book* must be carefully read."[2]

Dr. Baxter was a deep thinker, and his scholarly eloquence stands out in this classic work. How the parishioners in attendance at the Thursday evening lectures at Charlotte Chapel must have been blessed to *hear* this book spoken to them! The following sampling of *Explore the Book* should whet the appetite for further personal study.

> With all too many Christians today the tendency is to read the Bible just to pick up a few good points or suggestions for addressing meetings or preparing sermons, or to pick out a few nice bits to help with the Christian life. This is bad. It results in scrappiness. It engenders superficiality both mentally and spiritually. The word of God was never meant merely for these hurried consultations. We need to study and to know the written word of God as a whole, for such study and knowledge gives depth and richness and

fulness to *all* our public ministry, and stabilises our whole Christian experience. Moreover, I would remind fellow-preachers that the greatest sermons usually come when we are not looking for sermons but are studying the word of God for the sake of its own vital truth.[3]

In the studies which we here commence we approach the Bible as being in its totality *the Word of God*; and in all our studying of it, therefore, we are seeking to learn, under the illumination of the Holy Spirit, the mind and the truth and the will of God.

In our study of the Bible, also, we need ever to guard against becoming so engrossed in the fascination of the *subject* that we lose sight of the *object*. As we have said, in these studies we want to get hold of the big, broad meanings in the wonderful old Book: but unless the meanings get hold of *us* our study will have failed of its vital objective. Our Lord Jesus Himself has taught us that HE is the focal theme of all the Scriptures; and everywhere, therefore, we want to see beyond the *written* word, to Him who is the *living* Word. And we want to see Him in such a way as causes us to love and trust Him the more. Dr. Jowett tells of a tourist who was travelling through some of Scotland's loveliest scenery, but who was so absorbed in his guide book that he never saw the loveliness through which he was passing. There can be Bible study of that sort, too. Our great object is to know the true God, to become more like Christ, and to be more fully possessed by the Holy Spirit. True Bible study will encompass that object, for the inspired pages of Holy writ live and thrill and glow with the presence of God![4]

THE NEW TESTAMENT is the most vital book in the world. Its supreme *subject* is the Lord Jesus Christ. Its supreme *object* is the salvation of human beings. Its supreme *project* is the ultimate reign of the Lord Jesus in boundless and endless empire.

Christ is *the* subject of its pages. Is He not also the subject of the Old Testament? Yes, but not in the same way or with

the same exclusiveness. He who figures in the Old as the Christ of *prophecy* now emerges in the New as the Christ of *history*. He who is the super-*hope* of the Old is the super-*fact* of the New. Expectancy in the Old has become *experience* in the New. *Pre*vision has become *pro*vision. That which was latent has now become patent. The long-predicted is the now-presented.[5]

The best summation of *Explore the Book* is typified in Dr. Baxter's own words:

Structurally the New Testament is built together in the form of a literary *archway*. When one pauses to reflect on it there is no kind of edifice which so accurately expresses the spiritual function and significance of the New Testament as an archway. What are these twenty-seven documents, these collected memoirs and letters which comprise the New Testament, but a literary archway leading to something beyond themselves? Are they not, in their total union, God's

171

wonderfully constructed archway into saving truth, into the true knowledge of Himself, into eternal blessedness?[6]

Perhaps the life and works of J. Sidlow Baxter can also be likened to an archway—an archway that points and leads the way to heaven.

His Poems

One of the delights of J. Sidlow Baxter's life was to compose poetry. He could write a poem at the drop of a hat. Whether it was a loving tribute to a friend, an anniversary or birthday, or just to say "thank you" to the nurses who took care of him at the hospital, his gratitude would wax eloquently in poetic strains. The following previously unpublished poems fairly represent the poet in the man.

Love's Gentle Chivalry

How tender, sensitive is love!
No taloned eagle; a white dove.
Soft as a cherub's folded wing,
Sweet as the sound when angels sing,
Pure as the first primrose of Spring.
　　Love's epithet
　　Is "Give" not "Get".

No mailed glove, no tyrant heel,
No vengeful spite will love reveal;
Soon hurt, restored tho' sooner yet,
Good will remember, ill forget,
And scorn to pay revenge's debt.
　　The more love gives
　　The more it lives.

172

Yes, this is love's prerogative—
To give, and give, and give.[7]

JSB

Tornado! Cruelist, Deadliest Scare!

Tornado! Cruelest, deadliest scare!
Mad demon shrieking through the air
Foul plunderer of hearts and homes!
Fierce dragon-mouth that fumes and foams!
From somewhere in a galvanized air
But who on earth can say from where?
What wreckage oft he leaves behind!
What sorrow in the tortured mind!
Yet even greater than the whole
Are wild tornadoes of the *soul*!
When normal thought is torn apart
And chaos fags the mind and heart
And God and Christ seem deaf or dead
And prospects fill the soul with dread.
Ah, then, how blest the soul-relief
When God steps in to assuage our grief!
When with those everlasting arms
He lifts us o'er those dread alarms
And desolating doubts give way
To faith and hope and brighter day!
Yes God is Master of winds and sky,
Even tornados must obey.[8]

JSB

Operation Morning

(Operation not as early in morning as expected.
The following lines written in bed at hospital
while waiting to be taken to operating theatre.)

173

I'm as "fit as a fiddle",
I'm as light as a lark,
I'm as mild at my middle
As I'm bold round my bark.
No dread of the surgeons,
No "nerves" about knives!
I'm as "fit as a fiddle",
Or a cat with nine lives.

I'm as "fit as a fiddle",
I'm as sprightly as Spring;
So "Hey-diddle-diddle"
I smilingly sing.
"Tut tut" for the table;
No mopings for me;
I'm as happy this morning
As a Christian should be.[9]

JSB

A Love Problem

Two boys both loved a pretty maid,
    A damsel fair to see;
Each mind was hopeful yet afraid,
    And anxious as could be.

For ardent love demands return
    Within the loved one's heart.
Love's rapture-flame can never burn
    In lovers kept apart.

What pains each love-sick laddie racked!
    She must be his alone!
Love giv'n the other boy he lacked
    To satisfy his own!

174

But these two boys were bosom friends,
  And loved each other well;
And so to meet the other's ends
  Each tried his love to quell.

What inward pinings! What despair!
  What tumult all unseen!
Each day the maiden seemed more fair,
  Each day the pain more keen!

'Twas most unhappy, you'll agree,
  Each trying his love to hide;
The one way out was, as you see,
  THE MAIDEN MUST DECIDE![10]

JSB

His Other Books

J. Sidlow Baxter was in the habit of rising early. He rose at five o'clock each morning all his life, except when he turned ninety—he then rose at six o'clock. His self-sacrifice is seen in his prolific writing ministry.

Most of his books are out of print, but some fifteen to twenty can often be found on Internet sites that feature rare Christian books.

1) *Enter Ye In* (1939, Marshall, Morgan & Scott, Ltd.)

His first published book. He states in the foreword, "The messages in this little book have first been given as Sunday evening addresses from the pulpit of Charlotte Chapel, then used as printed articles in the twelve monthly tracts during 1939, and are now issued in this collective form with the earnest prayer that the Spirit of God may use them to bring souls to a saving knowledge of our Lord Jesus."[11] The

175

following is a sample from the first chapter entitled, "The Insistent Question."

SIMPLY BELIEVE!

See how *easy* God has made the way of salvation—"Believe on the Lord Jesus Christ and thou shalt be saved"! Nothing could be plainer or easier. None of those who perish will ever be able to allege that the way of salvation was not simple or easy enough. Faith is the primary and most elementary law of our nature. The first thing a babe does is to trust. The human babe is the most helpless of all new-born animals. It can do nothing but trust others. Faith is also the *last* thing with us. When age comes on, and our powers decline, and the feebleness of a spent and decrepit body leaves us unable to fend for ourselves, we must trust ourselves to others. Faith is a necessity, and is natural to us. God had graciously ordered that the necessities of life are very simple matters for us. We must eat; and even a blind man can find the way to his mouth. We must drink; and even a babe knows how to do this without any teaching. Faith is really just as simple and natural to us. God simply asks us to exercise toward Him that which we naturally exercise toward others. Trust of oneself to another is not a "problem" to the babe; nor is it any matter of peculiar and aggravating intricacy to the aged. Yet when we tell men that the salvation of the soul comes simply by trusting Christ, they begin to think this thing and the other about it until presently they make faith a most perplexing matter. What foolishness is this! Saving faith is just to take God at His word: simply to rest on the finished work of Christ. Why need we try to *explain* faith? Our very endeavours to explain it often becloud it rather than clarify it. The fact is, all human beings know quite well what it is to believe, or trust. No explainings are needed.

Are you seeking to be right with God, to be a saved soul, to be sure of forgiveness, to be set free from sin? Away then with all hindering suspicions that there is something mysterious or complicated about faith. Simply and naturally take God at His word. Simply and solely rest upon the finished work of Christ. Do not fall into the snare of looking for some strange new feeling to come over you. Look to Christ alone.[12]

2) *Mark These Men* (1949, Marshall, Morgan & Scott, Ltd.)

Dr. Baxter is at this point still relatively unknown in the United States. This book is a brief study of thirteen Bible characters. They are a compilation of Sunday morning messages he preached at Charlotte Chapel. The following is the introduction to a chapter entitled, "The Man Who Routed the Aliens."

Gideon, the fifth judge of Israel, is always counted—and rightly so—as one of the outstanding heroes in Israel's history. The eleventh chapter of the Epistle to the Hebrews includes him in its classic catalogue of Old Testament worthies who through faith wrought exploits; and I would be the last man to question his right to appear in that illustrious list. Yet if we are rightly to appraise Gideon, we need to realise at the outset that his heroism was not the product of his natural make-up, but the outcome of a transforming spiritual experience through which he passed. It is this which gives Gideon a living significance to ourselves today; for the transforming experience through which Gideon passed, we may pass through, and with an equally transforming result.[13]

In 1959, when J. Sidlow Baxter began to visit conferences and pulpits in America and Canada, his popularity also increased with the reading public. He had a close relationship with the Zondervan family, which lasted until 1983. The "Zondervan period" produced his richest legacy of works.

177

3) *Going Deeper* (1959, Zondervan)

This book established Dr. Baxter as a deep thinker and popular writer. Centered around the verse, Philippians 3:10, "That I may know him, and the power of his resurrection, and the fellowship of his sufferings, being made conformable unto his death." It is a powerful work and it has had a profound impact on its readers. The following is an introductory paragraph to a chapter entitled, "The Unseen Loved One."

So far, we have been speaking about *knowing* Christ; but by its very nature such a theme impels us onward to further territory. Knowing Him must be complemented by *loving* Him, for as the intellect finds in Him its supreme illumination and reward, so the heart finds in Him the perfectly delectable Object of its love. None can satisfy the outreaching of the human heart as He. The more we ponder this, the more luminous and certain it becomes. Others are but "broken lights" compared with Him. He is the sum and crown of all moral excellence, and therefore supremely loveable. It is said that "love is blind"; yet is it not they who say so who are blind? Love can see more through a tear-drop than Reason ever saw through a telescope or a microscope! To minds blinded by "the god of this age" our Lord may be merely a "root out of a dry ground", but to the opened eyes of faith and love He is "the fairest among ten thousand and the altogether lovely". Yet our love to Him must not be merely aesthetic or contemplative or sentimental; it must be the outreaching of active passion. It is in doing, not dreaming, that true love wings upward to its zenith of joy. In reality, love is not just affection, but devotion; and it reaches its highest expression, not in sympathy, but in sacrifice. True love to Christ is no mere mystical admiration, but a practical loyalty. Such love is what our Lord seeks from us more than all else. There is no substitute because there is no equivalent. Staggering though it sounds, it is true: He wants my love. When I love Him "with all my

178

heart and mind and soul and strength", then, and only then, does it become individually true of me, "He shall see of the travail of His soul and shall be satisfied."[14]

Zondervan brought out five publications of J. Sidlow Baxter in 1960 and each one was a jewel. One was a sensation, *Explore the Book*. One was a blockbuster, *Awake My Heart*. On the book flap, Dr. W. A. Criswell, pastor of First Baptist Church in Dallas, Texas, said of *Awake My Heart*, "One of the most spiritually exhilarating and homiletically refreshing experiences that any preacher or Bible student could enjoy is to read the published volumes of J. Sidlow Baxter. His expositions provide a fountain of preaching and teaching material that can be easily used in mediating the truth of God to others."

4) *Awake My Heart* (1960, Zondervan)

A critically acclaimed bestseller (over a million copies are in print), *Awake My Heart* was chosen in 1991 as a devotional book to be part of the president's study. Isa still reads a page of it every day, as do thousands of other Christians. The following is a sample devotional page:

HOLINESS UNTO THE LORD

"Ye shall be holy: for I the LORD your God am holy."—Lev. 19:2. The first five books of the Bible are all from the pen of Moses. They form a complete group, and are known as the Pentateuch. In Genesis we see *ruin* through the sin of man; in Exodus *redemption* through the power of God; in Leviticus *fellowship* on the ground of atonement; in Numbers *guidance* during pilgrimage; in Deuteronomy *destination* after completed discipline. In Genesis we see the divine *sovereignty*; in Exodus the divine *power*; in Leviticus the divine *holiness*; in Numbers the divine "*goodness and severity*"; in Deuteronomy the divine *faithfulness*.

179

Leviticus, the middle book of the five, is the divine call to holiness. God insists on the sanctification of His people. The book falls into two main parts. In chapters 1 to 17 all relates to the *tabernacle*; in chapters 18 to 27 all pertains to *character and conduct*. Part one shows the *way* to God—by sacrifice; part two shows the *walk* with God—by sanctification. Part one teaches us the propitiatory *basis* of fellowship with God; part two teaches the personal *behavior* which conditions fellowship with God. All the way through there rings the call to holiness. In part one the stipulation is *ceremonial and hygienic* purity; in part two it is *ethical and practical* sanctity in daily walk.

So then, the call to *practical* sanctification begins at chapter 18, and it speaks to God's people in every generation. It gives us the three basic reasons why we should be a holy people.

Reason number one is that *our God Himself is holy*. The chapter begins: "I am Jehovah your God. After the doings of the land of Egypt wherein ye dwelt ye shall not do; and after the doings of the land of Canaan whither I bring you shall ye not do. Ye shall do My judgments, and keep Mine ordinances, to walk therein: I am Jehovah your God."

Reason number two why we are to be a holy people is that *our High Priest is holy*. As the tabernacle was a threefold structure—outer court, holy place, and holy of holies, so the nation Israel was arranged in a three-fold way which corresponded, i.e. the congregation, the priesthood, and the high priest. Israel's sanctification reached its culminative representation in the high priest, who wore the golden crown invested with the words, "Holiness unto Jehovah". (See Lev. 21:12 with Exod. 28:36 and 29:6.) Even so, *our* dear and wonderful High Priest, the Lord Jesus, stands yonder in the *heavenly* temple, wearing the crown of perfect holiness, bearing our names as jewels upon His mighty shoulders and tender heart, the Representative of a spiritual Israel called to be "a peculiar people, zealous of good works". Oh, is not *that* a radiant,

180

sacred challenge to us to cleanse our hands and separate ourselves from unholy ways?

Reason number three why we are to be a holy people is that *the Spirit who indwells us is holy*. As the shekinah light shone above the mercy seat and between the arching wings of the two cherubim in the holy of holies (Exod. 25:22; Num. 7:89), so the divine Spirit indwells each of us who are blood-bought, covenant members of Christ, making us "temples of the living God" (1 Cor. 3:16; 6:19). Must we not as human sanctuaries of the *Holy* Spirit allow Him so to possess us and control us and suffuse us that all our words and works and ways are holy?[15]

5) *His Part and Ours* (1960, Zondervan)

A review of this book by *Moody Monthly*, quoted on the book jacket, states, "A most precious asset to any library. The keynote is the possessive 'my'. The author deals with rich kernels of religious truth. Six chapters present 'his part' as 'my redeemer,' etc., showing the believer's absolute, non-negotiable religious possessions. The Triune God is seen to be all that we need for every circumstance of time and eternity. Truly a great book."

6) *Studies in Problem Texts* (1960, Zondervan)

J. Sidlow Baxter was forever digging into the Bible's meanings and interpretations. *Studies in Problem Texts* takes the reader to the problematic texts in Scripture where Dr. Baxter uncovers no problem at all. Tackling such controversial subjects as the "Sons of God" from Genesis 6, to the "Unpardonable Sin" of Matthew 12, Dr. Baxter takes his readers on a journey whereby seemingly difficult passages are clearly explained. In his foreword he writes,

We never get to the end of the Bible. It is as wise in its reservations as in its revelations. Enough is revealed to

181

make faith intelligent. Enough is reserved to give faith scope for development. Everything needful to salvation and godliness is written with such clarity that all the simple-hearted may understand; but there are other matters which, with wise divine purpose, are presented less lucidly, or even enigmatically, so as to challenge enquiry—matters fascinating, mysterious, or more intricate, but all yielding rich and sanctifying reward to devout exploration.[16]

7) *For God So Loved* (1960, Zondervan)

An in-depth look at John 3:16, *For God So Loved* is a rich exposition that focuses on the ten main words of the verse. It contains a practical exposition that is easily understood. To prove this point, in the foreword he tells of a man who was saved by reading this little book. He writes, "Some years ago, when this book was first published, a lady who had an appointment with a dental surgeon, over in England, sat reading it while waiting for her appointment. Unintentionally, on leaving, she left it behind. The dentist picked it up, read it, and as a result received God's wonderful gift, became truly saved and a rejoicing Christian."[17]

8) *A New Call to Holiness* (1967, Marshall, Morgan, & Scott, Ltd.)

9) *His Deeper Work in Us* (1967, Marshall, Morgan, & Scott, Ltd.)

10) *Our High Calling* (1967, Marshall, Morgan, & Scott, Ltd.)

Known as the "Christian Sanctification Series," these three stellar works are the product of a man who lived it as well as wrote it. Sid used to tell Isa to read a book first once, then twice, then three times to learn it well. One would do well to read each book in this series three times for its contents to sink in. They are not "easy reads." In the first volume, *A New Call to Holiness*, he lays the groundwork on what Scripture says about personal holiness. In volume two, *His Deeper Work in Us*, he gives a "how-to" approach to inward sanctification. In volume three, *Our High Calling*, he speaks at length on how to completely surrender to Christ minute by minute. In the last paragraph of his foreword to *A New Call to Holiness*, he writes, "In this connection, it is my persuasion that the Bible is trying to say something fresh to us again today on the deeply important, sacredly sensitive matter of Christian sanctification; and in these studies I ask the reader to *listen* with me—to catch the accents of *a new call to holiness* as that living voice from heaven speaks again through the written Word. Let our prayer be, 'Speak, Lord, for Thy servant heareth'."[18]

11) *Does God Still Guide?* (1971, Marshall, Morgan, and Scott, Ltd.)

Baxter's little gem of a book, *Does God Still Guide?*, stands as one of his best works. What could be more important to a Christian than one's prayer life? In this book Dr. Baxter creates a "how-to" manual on prayer. He states that "guidance and prayerlessness never go together."[19]

In his chapter, "How Do We Know Guidance?", he states,

> How may we *recognize* divine guidance when it comes? How may we distinguish it from the merely seeming? That is an important question. In reality, however, the criteria of true guidance are easily perceivable. To begin with, here are three detector-tests of the false.

First, true guidance is *never contrary to Scripture*. If any seemingly expedient course of action contradicts any clear teaching of the written Word, then it is branded thereby as wrong. The Holy Spirit in the *child* of God never contradicts Himself in the *Word* of God.

Second, true guidance is *never contrary to plain duty*. If a seemingly guided procedure evades moral obligation, or violates honest principle, then it is spurious guidance. The Holy Spirit never contradicts the believer's conscience.

Third, true guidance is *never contrary to highest reason*. When the pressure to do something is impatient, impetuous, flurrying, or urges sudden or risky action without due reflection, it is counterfeit. Although divine guidance may sometimes *transcend* sanctified human intelligence, it never *collides* with it.

But now, how may we recognise *true* guidance? Well, in this connection it is instructive to review divine methods of guidance in times past. In the camp of Israel guidance was threefold:

1. The pillar of cloud and fire (Exod. 13:21, Neh. 9:19).
2. The blowing of the trumpets (Num. 10:1–9).
3. The use of Urim and Thummin (Exod. 28:30, Lev. 8:8, etc.). The first was guidance to the *eye*. The second was guidance to the *ear*. The third was exceptional guidance for particular episodes. The first two were outward and general; the third was inner and special. . . .

Moreover, in the New Testament the *instruments* of guidance change. No more the pillar or trumpets, the Urim and Thummim . . . there are now the new teachings of Jesus, also the new and divinely inspired Scriptures of the Church; and all these are illumined by the Holy Spirit in each individual Christian believer. . . . Here it is: divine guidance comes by (1) the written Word of God, (2) the inward urge of the Spirit, (3) indication by outward circumstance. These three are not only the *means* of divine guidance; they are the *tests* of it.[20]

12) *The Master Theme of the Bible* (1973, Tyndale)

This book's central theme is the sovereignty and revelation of Jesus Christ as the Lamb of God. Dr. Baxter states in his foreword his intention for the readers of this book: "In both the preaching and the writing of these reflections, the subject has set my own heart singing with new love and gratitude to our inexpressibly glorious Savior-King, and my longing is that at least some other hearts may be moved to love and prize him more earnestly through the reading of this book."[21]

13) *The Strategic Grasp of the Bible* (1974, Zondervan)

For those readers who are intimidated by the size of *Explore the Book*, this condensed version of that work is reduced to 406 pages. It surveys the structure and panorama of the Bible while offering stimulating comparisons between the Old and New Testaments.

14) *Rethinking Our Priorities* (1974, Zondervan)

There were few topics more important to J. Sidlow Baxter than worship and pulpit preaching. It grieved his heart to see the deterioration of truth taught from the pulpit as well as the replacement of the "old hymns" with more contemporary music. In this book, Dr. Baxter challenges churches to return to a more "traditional" mode of church service, with more emphasis placed on prayer and spirit-lifting hymns. To gain a full understanding of J. Sidlow Baxter, one must understand his strong ideas and principles on church worship. *Rethinking Our Priorities* was a clarion call for evangelical churches in America to return to their halcyon years.

He begins this challenging book with a "letter of introduction":

Dear Pastor, Music leader, Officeholder, Church member: Never did I let a book slip through the press to the public with more diffidence. It is not easy to write things which may severely displease. There is in each of us an inborn self-protectiveness which prefers the "safety of our own skin"; and some of you may think that I should be "skinned alive" for things written in part three of this book, i.e., my critique of public worship in the evangelical churches of America. Those of you who are my brethren in the ministry may find provocative jolts, also, in part one; but I am brave enough to hope you *will*!

I am comforted to think that all of you who know me or my books will know that I am not a disgruntled old grumbler "agin everybody." I love my brethren in the ministry and my fellow evangelicals too well for that. But I am concerned deeply to see some wrongs put right for the sake of the cause which is supremely dear to all of us.[22]

15) *Divine Healing of the Body* (1979, Zondervan)

A tender, personal look into the emotions of J. Sidlow Baxter, *Divine Healing of the Body* contains candid talk about his diabetes and his wife Ethel's bout with cancer. Ethel died before the manuscript was published. Dr. Baxter opens his heart for all the world to see how Jesus became nearer and dearer during this grief-stricken time in his life. He also takes a historical look at divine healings and presents current testimonies of other individuals who claimed God healed them. He addresses the persistent problem: why are some healed and others not?

16) *Daily Wings* (1983, Zondervan)

This devotional book contains Dr. Baxter's original hymns and poems. The popularity of hymns and poems had waned and the poor reception the book received was a great disappointment to Dr. Baxter. Perhaps because of its poor sales, his long business relationship with Zondervan ended with this book. Written as a devotional, it was hoped to become another *Awake My Heart*. It did not. It is a shame, for it is a well-written book that displays the talents of Dr. Baxter as a poet and hymnodist.

17) *Majesty, The God You Should Know* (1984, Here's Life Publishers)

The sales of Dr. Baxter's books from this point forward would never match his previous efforts. *Majesty* is a series of lectures compiled for publication, and it is a wonderful book on God and how to know him personally. In the opening paragraph he writes,

> God is the greatest of all mysteries and the greatest of all realities. He is the infinite mystery behind all reality, and the absolute reality behind all mystery; unimaginably exceeding the profoundest grasp of human comprehension, and beyond all verbal definition. Neither the phenomenal universe nor the invisible universe of thought has any satisfactory explanation apart from God, but the being of God Himself is utterly beyond explanation. He immeasurably outbounds the most distant reach of stars and space in all directions, yet He is so exquisitely close to each of us as to be, in Tennyson's phrase, "closer than breathing, nearer than hands and feet." He is the one "in whom we live and move and have our being," the God "in whose hand our breath is"; the Infinite who fills everywhere. Before all other being began, God already was, or rather, eternally *is*. When He created the universe, He added nothing to Himself, and as He still creates amid His universe adds nothing to Himself, for to the Infinite nothing can be added.[23]

18) *The Hidden Hand* (1985, Living Books Publishers)

This is a beautifully written novel, his only one. It is autobiographical to a degree (only he knew to which degree). *The Hidden Hand* is a carefully woven story of love, despair, tragedy, and hope. Afraid that it might not sell, Baxter bought five thousand copies and sold them himself.

19) *The Other Side of Death* (1987, Tyndale)

J. Sidlow Baxter never shied away from controversy. In this, his last published book, Baxter examines what the Bible says about life beyond death. In it he cries out against the "soul sleep theory" espoused by E. W. Bullinger. There is a section of the book devoted to our departed Christian loved ones. He also dispels the idea of purgatory and speaks at length about heaven and hell. In the foreword he states the premise for the book.

> No apology need ever be made for publishing an honest contribution to the subject of death and the Beyond. However big and pressing the questions related to our present short life on earth may seem, they shrink into littleness compared with this timeless, measureless concern of death and the hereafter. How long earthly life looks to questing youth! How quickly fled it seems to the aged! The grandfather clock ticks away the minutes so slowly, but in retrospect the years seem to have scurried away like dust before a gale. No matter how wise a man may think himself, if he neglects to enquire as to the long, long journey which he must soon take on the other side of death he is a fool. That millions of people can treat the matter with jaunty indifference must be an astonishment to angels and demons.[24]

His Hymns

What a void there would be in Christian literature and worship if we did not have the book of Psalms. From the extremes of desperation to adulation, King David poured out his heart to God in psalms. Like King David, J. Sidlow Baxter poured out his heart in hymns to his Creator. One of the great joys of his life was to compose and sing hymns to the Lord. One of the great disappointments of his life was to see the popularity of hymns in evangelical churches in America wane and be replaced by contemporary music. He tried later in life to get a book of his original hymns published. To his dismay, the publisher asked him to put up the money! His book of hymns never made it to press. Nevertheless, Dr. Baxter still kept writing hymns up till his death. At age ninety-six he was asked by the committee in England celebrating the life of C. S. Lewis to write the words for the hymn to be sung at the closing of every session. Dr. Baxter frequently quoted the hymns of Wesley and Cowper. He believed the "old hymns" helped to carry one's spirit upward to the heavens while honoring God with worship and praise. The following are a couple of his hymns:

> HERE we praise the God of grace;
> Here we seek the Saviour's face;
> Here our heartfelt love we sing,
> To our dear Redeemer-King.
> Hearts aglow with grateful joy,
> Come, let praise be our employ;
> Let us swell our praises high,
> Till they echo in the sky.
> Christ the Lord has made us free;
> He has made our eyes to see;
> He has healed the lame and weak,
> Giv'n the dumb the power to speak.

He has giv'n the deaf to hear,
By His love has cast out fear.
Wondrous grace! Our praise, begun,
Never, never shall be done.

All in Christ are richly blest;
All in Him find peace and rest;
Poor in spirit find great wealth,
Sin-sick souls find life and health.
Here the contrite, bowed with grief,
Find a sweet and full relief.
Matchless love! With hearts aflame,
Shall we not extol His Name?

Oh, the debt of love we owe!
Well His wondrous grace we know.
Stronger His great love than death,
Constant as our very breath.

Here our heartiest praise is faint;
Yonder, free from earth's restraint,
Zion's hills with songs we'll ring,
Deathless praises to our King.[25]

JSB

Sanctify me wholly,
    Sovereign Saviour mine:
Spirit, soul and body
    Now make fully Thine.
Make my motives blameless,
    Purify my heart;
Set me now entirely
    For Thyself apart.

Thou to this dost call me,
    In Thy written word;
Thou Thyself wilt do it,
    If I trust Thee, Lord.
Faithful is Thy calling
    And Thy promise too;
Give me now to trust Thee,
    And to prove Thee true.

Here and now I yield, Lord,
    Thine to be alone;
Now is "Self" uncrowned, Lord,
    Thou dost take the throne.
Ever keep and fill me,
    Pour through me Thy grace;
Till, at Thine appearing,
    I behold Thy face.[26]

JSB

twelve

THE OCTOGENARIAN

In the day when the keepers of the house shall tremble,
and the strong men shall bow themselves, and the grinders
cease because they are few, and those that look out of the
windows be darkened.

ECCLESIASTES 12:3

His Biblical Diet

In 1513 the Spanish explorer Ponce de León wandered
through swampland off the east coast of Florida in a vain
search for the fabled "fountain of youth." In 1521 he died
from mortal wounds received from the Calusa Indians—
perishing without discovering the eternal spring. J. Sidlow
Baxter was not just an octogenarian but a nonagenarian,
living to be two months shy of his ninety-seventh birthday. Did Dr. Baxter possess a longevity secret? Perhaps,
for he claimed God ordered his people to eat only certain

things. He was a vegetarian who occasionally ate certain fish. His wife, Isa, is a vegetarian and is careful what she eats as well—she is very vibrant at age ninety-seven. At the grocery store he carefully read each item before purchase to weed out those with added preservatives and chemical agents. He shied away from white flour, red meat, and all processed foods.

Baxter believed what the Bible taught about eating and diet and he lived his life by what the Bible said. He spoke at length about this Biblical diet in his wonderful book *Our High Calling*. Joyce Rogers, wife of Adrian Rogers of Bellevue Baptist Church, wrote a book based on a Biblical diet. She mentions J. Sidlow Baxter more than once as one who profoundly influenced her. She states,

> Dr. J. Sidlow Baxter was a wonderful Bible teacher and author who has had a great influence on my life spiritually. He was also a follower of good nutrition and a healthful lifestyle in general. He was in his nineties when he died, and he maintained a tremendous quality of life into his old age. The following is a summary statement of his philosophy of the proper way of eating. He practiced biblical principles for many years.[1]
>
> How important is proper diet! How many thousands today are in our overcrowded hospitals who never would have been there but for wrong eating! How many have inadvertently committed slow suicide with their knives and forks! Many of us have so perverted and enslaved our palates by devitalized taste-tickling dainties and savories, that to eat food just as Nature supplies it now seems abnormal!
>
> With my Bible open before me I would say to all: keep off meat with the blood still in it. Keep off animal fats. Keep off all parts of the hog. Keep off all those forbidden land creatures and finless aquatic creatures which the Mosaic law disallows. Keep away as much as possible from white bread, white sugar, white rice. Look carefully at the

wrapped, packaged or canned foodstuffs which you buy at the grocery stores. Keep away from all those sugary breakfast cereals which tell you the vitamins or minerals which the manufacturer has injected, but do not tell you all the vital elements which have been eliminated.

Even if it costs more, get guaranteed whole-wheat bread; and as a cereal get pure wheat germ. Let the milk which you buy be that which is least artificially treated. Guard against buying those eating commodities which are marked as containing chemical preservatives, also those which have artificial flavorings and colourings.[2]

In *Our High Calling*, Dr. Baxter has an entire chapter dedicated to the subject of diet. Entitled "Sanctification and the Diet Law," the chapter covers the Mosaic Law and its relation to born-again Christians in regard to diet. He diffuses the argument for pork consumption by those who interpret Acts 10 (Peter's vision of the sheet of unclean animals) to mean that God has done away with the old dietary restrictions of the Mosaic Law. He comments, "To argue from Acts 10 that the Gospel now makes unclean beasts and birds and creeping things clean, or that the re-generation of our *souls* alters the digestive organs of our *bodies*, or that the glad tidings of salvation by grace annul the divine diet-code of good health through clean eating, is to grab at the wind."[3] One either agrees or disagrees with Baxter's theory on the dietary code. However, he did live to be almost ninety-seven by sticking to this diet!

J. Sidlow Baxter had learned firsthand what dangerous paths lay ahead for those who disobey God's directives. When he went against the Bible's warnings of consuming much honey, he eventually ended up in the emergency room of Cottage Hospital in Santa Barbara with acute diabetes. There was no other instance of diabetes in the Baxter family in either his father's or mother's line. In his

194

case it was unwittingly self-induced. He consumed honey so frequently that his flesh began to sag and he had a pasty look about him.

He relates the story in *Divine Healing of the Body*,

> I had an insatiable thirst and could not help drinking, drinking, drinking at the cold water tap; yet all the while I seemed to be drying up. I went thin and looked haggard. "Oh, Mrs. Baxter," a neighbor volunteered, "your husband has all the symptoms of diabetes!"
>
> Yes, I had brought on diabetes. For five years and more I had so continuously over-sugared myself that at last my bewildered little pancreas had cried, "Sid, old boy, I just cannot take any more! I'll have to spill all this sugar over into your system!" The result: Diabetes melitus!
>
> I wished I had known my Bible a bit better. Twice in one chapter we are warned: "It is not good to eat much honey" (Prov. 25:27, cf. v. 16).[4]

From 1965 on, J. Sidlow Baxter paid attention to what the Bible said about diet. It paid off. In a video of him celebrating his ninetieth birthday, he is a man who appears to be in his seventies. He is vibrant, energetic, and exudes vigor. So what did he eat? For breakfast he loved buckwheat pancakes or porridge. Occasionally he would "mahsh a bahnanah" and place it on a piece of whole-wheat toast with peanut butter and a *touch* of honey and have that for breakfast. For lunch he would have soup—mainly vegetable. He loved the soups Isa made for him. For dinner he ate vegetables with fish. His favorite meal out was the tuna sandwich at the Red Lion in Santa Barbara. He would eat cheese and milk.

There are critics who argue that the Bible is an outdated book with little practical advice for the "modern man." J. Sidlow Baxter lived by the Bible. He lived by its spiritual laws and its dietary laws.[5] For him the Bible was a handbook on all aspects of life and how to live that life more abundantly.

> I know the problem of keeping rigidly to this in these days; but do it as far as is possible, remembering always that one of the indispensable ways of keeping healthy is to eat *live* foods, fresh and untampered with, as Nature gave them. To offset the more or less devitalized foods which you perhaps cannot *altogether* avoid at the modern grocer's, eat regularly plenty of fresh vegetables, fruits, grains and nuts. I am not a vegetarian but I acknowledge only too willingly that even when there is little or no flesh-meat in one's diet, that lack is negligible if sufficient nuts and grains are included. Indeed, such is the protein value of the soybean and certain others as to make flesh meat practically unnecessary. *Un*processed cheeses, and especially *cottage* cheese, are wonderfully rich, also, in proteins.
>
> How many a life of gifted and powerful ministry has been cut short by inattention to these things! Christian sanctification let us never forget, has undoubted reference to the *body*. Let every Christian see to it that the *body* is given proper food, and sufficient *exercise* such as suits our years, and sufficient rest in *sleep*. Many who are now far from well in body, and therefore often depressed in mind, would cure themselves and enjoy restoration to untroubled slumber far sooner than they think, if only they would resolutely observe the foregoing safeguards, all of which have Scriptural authentification.
>
> However, I will add no more, lest I should wander out of my own special province into that of the nutritionist or other physiological specialist. I cannot do better than conclude by saying: Observe the God-given dietary code of Mosaic Law; eat *good* food; keep active; rest regularly; . . . I am sure that such care, under such guidance, can spare us many ailments, lesser or worse, and engender years of continuing health, vigour, buoyancy, usefulness.[6]

Last known photo of J. Sidlow Baxter taken by his beloved Isa at Christmas about two months prior to his ninety-seventh birthday. As was his custom, he always wore a tie and often wore his favorite red tartan vest from Scotland.

It should be noted that upon Dr. Baxter's death, a drawer in his desk revealed he took vitamins. There were ten bottles in the drawer. He was taking magnesium, copper, and grape seed extract, to name a few. A friend of his commented that Dr. Baxter was constantly popping vitamins. It was obvious that he believed in maintaining his vessel for the Lord.

thirteen

THE PRAYING SAINT

And in the morning, rising up a great while before day, he went out, and departed into a solitary place, and there prayed.

MARK 1:35

His Prayer Life

Following in the footsteps of Jesus, J. Sidlow Baxter, too, rose early in the morning—5 a.m. for most of his life. It was his time spent in prayer that made him stand out among his peers. It was often said of his preaching, that one got the impression he had just left the throne room of God before stepping into the pulpit. He believed that a Christian's relationship with Jesus was only as good as the amount of time he spent in communion with him. Dr. Baxter spent much time in prayer, for it had become a habit with him.

It had not always been that way. Early on he struggled to develop a prayer time, battling with "his will." He would go in to pray and "will" would say, "no." Sometimes he would win and have a victorious prayer time; other times "will" would win and keep him from prayer. Until finally, he told "will" he was going in to pray and that was all there was to it. Then, "will" said, "I will join you." It was a clear victory over self and one of the secrets to his success as a Christian. Dr. Baxter used to say, "I can promise you if you study the great preachers you will find that all of them had a strong prayer life."

He examines the topic of prayer in his book *Does God Still Guide?*

> I asked myself: Which comes first, religious service?—or knowing God? Which has the *basic* importance: what I do?—or what I *am*? Which means more, both to God and men: quantity?—or *quality*? Which means more to Christ: my work for Him?—or my prayerful *love* for Him? In Christian life and service, which is the *utterly* vital: ability, activity?—or inwrought holiness of character? What would my reactions be about all these things (I asked myself) when at last I should meet my heavenly Master? Would I be meeting a Master whom I recognised by His incomparable splendour, but did not know personally (having been too busy serving)?—or would I at last be meeting face to face One whom I had for years known heart to heart?
>
> With startling newness it became clear to me that *all* those "first priorities" which give richest meaning to life are dependent upon and determined by the place we give to *prayer*.[1]

Dr. Baxter often remarked that *nothing* can be more important to a Christian's life and well-being than regular prayer. Isa remarked that early in the morning she would hear him in his study with the door closed, crying out to

God in an audible voice. He would pray throughout the day. At mealtimes, he and Isa prayed together. He kept a yellow sheet of paper which was folded to section out different prayer needs. One section had names of countries and missionaries in those countries. On Sundays he spent the day mainly in prayer for all the missionaries and countries on his list.

J. Sidlow Baxter loved Jesus and he desired to spend as much time as possible in fellowship with him. If any one thing can typify his distinguishable life, it has to be his prayer life. That was the well where he drew up his buckets of expository preaching and anointed messages. It was there, on his knees with his Bible and alone with the Creator of the universe, where his power lay. He had emptied himself so entirely that he could be flooded to the brim with the Divine Presence. That was the secret to his success in the pulpit—it lay in his prayer time with God.

Baxter detailed four levels of prayer.

In the Bible there seem to be *four levels* of prayer indicated. It is (1) a necessity, (2) a duty, (3) a privilege, (4) a delight. On the first level, prayer is simply but sheerly a *necessity*. Without it godliness withers and the spiritual life atrophies. What air is to the lungs, or oxygen to bodily health, prayer is to our spiritual development. Even Bible knowledge becomes stale and lifeless apart from prayer, just as even a well-fed body ails and dies without fresh air. Observation convinces me that whatever uplifting visitations or sanctifying experiences may come to us at one time or another, none ever becomes continuous in our spiritual life apart from regular, unhurried, secret prayer-time. Prayerlessness is a spiritual grave.

But there is that higher level on which prayer is seen as a moral *duty*. As an expression of worship it is our duty to *God*. As a means of intercession it is our duty to *others*. As a means of sanctification it is a duty to *ourselves*.

Because prayer is a duty, prayerlessness is sin. That is why Samuel said, "God forbid that I should *sin* against the Lord in ceasing to pray for you" (1 Sam.12:23). That aspect of prayerlessness as *sin* may well startle many of us.

Then there is the third level: prayer as a transcendent *privilege*. It gives access to the highest of all thrones, through the costliest of all sacrifices, with the readiest of all welcomes. There is no longer need to limp there in prodigals' rags; we are welcomed there as "sons of God" reinstated through the redeeming blood of Calvary. Our access never varies with our own fluctuating condition; it remains constant because it is on the basis of a finished atonement and an immutable covenant and an ever-efficacious Cross and an ever-prevailing Name. That such an all-eclipsing privilege can be treated indifferently by us must be an astonishment to angels!

But the highest level is when prayer becomes our dearest *delight*, opening up to us a heart-to-heart communion with God which is heaven begun below. So long as prayer is regarded as no higher than a necessity, a duty, or even as the loftiest of all privileges, it can never have its richest, loveliest meaning in our life. But when it has become a pure *delight*, a rapturous resort, a bliss of communion, a spontaneous heart-cry of holy desire, then we know not only the intercessory power of prayer but its exquisite inward reward.[2]

There was a fifth level which Dr. Baxter spoke of from the pulpit: a deeper form of prayer at the level of *absorption*. It was readily apparent to all who knew J. Sidlow Baxter that his prayer life was indeed a delight mixed with absorption.

J. Sidlow Baxter had developed the habit of prayer. He knew that his faith was based not on a religion but on a relationship with Jesus. And it was that relationship with his risen Lord that drew him to prayer more than anything else in life. He simply delighted to be in the company of Jesus. Dr. Baxter had a set discipline for prayer and he made his time in prayer productive. The following is his advice on how to pray effectively:

First: this is a good usual order: (1) express worship and adoration to God; (2) then express thanksgiving for all your many blessings: see Philippians 4:6, (3) intercede for others, whose names you have on a written list, (4) then pray for yourself, your deepest needs and longings. This order saves our prayer-times from deadly egocentricity and from interminable mere "asking".

Second: preface your praying by briefly meditating on a passage of Scripture. For this it is good to be going through the Gospels or some Epistle—a paragraph or so a day.

Third: pray steadily through an Epistle; so many verses each day; turning every exhortation, every challenge, every promise, every warning, into a prayer for its operation in your own life. This can make your prayer-hour so rich, it will be much too short! You will begrudge every merciless tick of the clock!

Fourth: use your hymn book. Make a list of all the best prayer-hymns, and *pray* them. Some of them will so surprise you and draw you out in longing prayer that you will keep coming back to re-pray them. Pray till your spiritual experience is up to the level of our best hymns.

To the foregoing simple recommendations I would add just two or three more. First, let intercession for *others* claim a large part of your praying. Paul did (Rom. 1:9, Eph. 1:16, Phil. 1:4, Col. 1:9, 1 Thess. 1:2). Many of us would find new liberation from captivity to trial, doubt, problems, if we prayed more for others and less for ourselves. Remember Job 42:10. "And the Lord turned the captivity of Job when he prayed for *his friends*"—not for himself [Baxter's emphasis]!

Do not over-complicate your prayer-life with too many subject-divisions. You are coming to a FATHER, not an accountant. Yet on the other hand *do* have some simple but sufficient system. In my own missionary praying I have found

203

it useful to have a map of the world sectioned into a weekly cycle. Use *written* memos and names. A Chinese proverb says, "the strongest memory is weaker than the weakest ink."

Always have one part of your prayer-period for *silent listening*. It is good that much of our praying should be in either outwardly or inwardly spoken words; but there is a language of the soul too deep for actual words. There is also a *silence* before God which speaks even *more* deeply—and at the same time *hears* God as only silence can. Remember young Samuel's words, "Speak, Lord, for Thy servant *heareth*" (1 Sam. 3:9,10 [Baxter's emphasis]). Some of us tend continually to transpose it: "Hear, Lord, for Thy servant speaketh." Practise *listening*! Never forget that last, sevenfold call of the Bible: "He that hath ears to *hear*, let him hear what the *Spirit* saith to the Churches" (Rev. 2:7 [Baxter's emphasis]). God needs listeners as well as pleaders.

What a subject is this matter of prayer! What books have been written on it through the centuries! What meaning it has had in the redeeming purpose of God and the sanctifying of the saints![3]

Fortunate were the individuals who landed on the prayer list of J. Sidlow Baxter. He was faithful in prayer and God honored that faithfulness. There is a story about H. D. McCarty knocking upon the Baxters' hotel room door; when the door was opened he realized he had interrupted their morning prayer time, whereby Dr. Baxter replied, "Oh, do come in, we were just having a spot of prayer!" And then Sid resumed his prayer, "Now, Lord, as I was saying before Harvey arrived . . ."

His Persistent Theme

J. Sidlow Baxter loved to preach on sanctification and holiness. And if ever there was a singular trait that stood out in his Christian life, it was his set-apartness and holiness to the Lord. He lived for the holy, he longed for the holy, he loved the holy. Like a mountain stream whose continual flow is derived from the melting snow that trickles down from its lofty peaks, J. Sidlow Baxter was gushing with living water he wished to share with others. He had found victory in the Christian life. Having appropriated by faith the Holy Spirit to renew his mind and create in him a desire for the holy things of God, he discovered that his baser desires were starved off and replaced with desires for the things of God. This was sanctification to him. He stood alone mostly on his interpretation of Scripture regarding the deeper life. He discusses the two camps that comprise the holiness theory in *A New Call to Holiness*.

Of holiness theories there are especially *two* which have long held sway; and still today, wherever the holiness emphasis remains, either one or the other is preached as the true "way of holiness"—not perhaps with the same dogmatism as formerly, yet just as decidedly. I am convinced that *both* theories are wrong. Both of them have brought wonderful promise of deliverance from indwelling sin, and both have brought thousands into later bondage. If we are again to see a revival of Christian believers rejoicing in the authentic experience of inward sanctification, the New Testament message (so I believe) must be rescued from these two impressive but subversive theories.

One of them is known as the "*eradication* theory"; the other as the "*counteraction* theory". Maybe many younger Christians today are unfamiliar with those expressions. None the less, all need to know what is represented by them, so as to be guarded from error and guided to the real truth.

The Eradication Theory

Take the first of them; that which we call the *eradication* theory. Ever since the venerable John Wesley formulated it, this doctrine has been widely promulgated all over the Christian world, and still is. The teaching is, that in "entire sanctification", which comes by the way of the "second blessing", there is complete eradication of "inbred sin", of the sinful "old man" or "old nature" or "the flesh", or the "carnal nature" which still lingers in the believer after conversion. The teaching is based on texts such as Romans 6:6, which, in our Authorized Version reads, "Our old man is crucified with Him (Christ) that the body of sin might be destroyed."[4]

So the eradication theory is: having yielded all to Christ we are by faith to identify ourselves with Him in His death, believing that our "old nature" is "crucified with Him" and "destroyed." Thenceforth we are to "reckon" ourselves "dead indeed unto sin"; and if we do, then the "reckoning" of ourselves dead to sin will become actual *experience* of it.[5]

The Counteraction Theory

. . . As we now touch on that other theory which we mentioned, i.e. the teaching that inward sanctification is effected, not by an eradication of our inherited sin-bias, but by a powerful counteraction of it. The counteraction theory is meant as an alternative to that of eradication.

There is little difference, really, between the "counteraction" theory and what used to be called the "*suppression*" theory (i.e. that although the sin-bias cannot be eradicated it can be thoroughly suppressed). The "counteraction" form of presentation is an exegetical amplification of the other, and has often been referred to as the *Keswick* theory.

Let this be clearly grasped: the "counteraction" theory denies eradication, and teaches victory over our hereditary sinfulness rather than complete freedom from it. It holds that the way of sanctification is by the counteraction-effect of an *inward joint-crucifixion with Christ*, and by "the law of the Spirit of life in Christ Jesus".[6]

We ourselves believe that both theories are just as wrong as they are sincere—as we shall respectfully endeavor to show.

. . . Let me state here, without waiting, our central thesis in these studies. It may be concentrated thus: *The inwrought sanctification of Christian believers is effected, not by a (supposed) inward union with our Lord Jesus in His crucifixion-death, but by full union with Him in His resurrection-life.*[7]

. . . We may learn much from our own English word, "sanctification", which is an excellent translation of the Greek original. Our word, "sanctification" comes from two Latin words—*sanctus*, which means "sacred" or "apart"; and *facio* which means "I make". So *sanctus* and *facio* together mean, "I make sacred", or "I set apart". That is the precise meaning of "sanctification". To be sanctified means to be set apart. In a Christian sense, it means to be set apart to Christ. In both the literal and the practical sense, entire sanctification is complete set-apartness to Christ.[8]

J. Sidlow Baxter typified the term sanctification, for his life was one set apart for Christ. For a deeper study of his views on holiness and sanctification, one should read his trilogy: *A New Call to Holiness, His Deeper Work in Us*, and *Our High Calling*.

fourteen

THE HEAVENLY HOMECOMING

And Moses was an hundred and twenty years old when he died: his eye was not dim, nor his natural force abated.

DEUTERONOMY 34:7

His Death

While in Texas one year, J. Sidlow Baxter came down with the flu during a preaching engagement. That particular flu bug laid him and Ethel low for a few days—to the degree that he wrote a poem about it.

> Two Texas flu bugs met one day,
> And someone overheard them say,
> "Aha, young preacher Sid draws nigh,
> Come, let us bug him: let him die!
> In fact we'll get young Ethel too;

We'll give them both our witch's brew!"
Poor Sid, he shook with such a cough,
It nearly carried him right off!

Yet in their naughty bombing raid
A strange mistake those flu bugs made;
The female bug, for Ethel meant,
Dived wide, and into Sid it went!
And thus, the genders being wrong,
Poor Sid kept preaching far too long.
His hearers thought he'd never stop
Unless, exhausted, he would flop!

However, that is all now past:
This evening's meeting is the last:
At dawn we leave for Salt Lake City.
And there, with neither tears nor pity,
Those Texas flu bugs we will take
And plunge them in the Mormon lake!
Then, after that, we're going home,
Resolving never more to roam!

JSB & EB (MAY 1975)

In December 1999 the Baxter home in Santa Barbara
was invaded with the flu bug. This time Isa got it. Then
the medical worker who stayed evenings got it. Then Sid
got it. His flu worsened and developed into pneumonia.
He was taken from his home to Mission Terrace Nursing
Home and just one day after his arrival, he went home to
be with the Lord on December 28, 1999.

Prophetically, in his novel, *The Hidden Hand*, he writes of
his own death due to pneumonia in the month of December.
Perhaps it was because he spent his life living on the doorstep
of heaven that he saw his future demise so clearly.

In the pulpit Sid often teased, "In regard to the rapture
of the Saints, I myself would prefer to die before that happy

event comes. I want to die first because that way I will have Jesus *all* to myself on that day. You see, there will be such a *crowd* at the rapture." J. Sidlow Baxter got his wish just two months shy of his ninety-seventh birthday.

His Memorial Services

On January 5, 2000, his friends gathered to pay tribute to the man who had so touched their lives. His memorial service was held at the Welch-Rice-Haider Chapel in Santa Barbara, California. Isa was comforted by the love of her late husband's friends. Dr. H. D. McCarty, senior pastor of University Baptist Church in Fayetteville, Arkansas, delivered the memorial message. And Dr. Harold Bussell, senior pastor of El Montecito Presbyterian Church in Montecito, California, performed the reading of Scripture and prayer.

Dr. Al Silvera, a friend of Sid's, eulogized him with the following words:

> From the time I first heard the story, I have wished I could have been one of the Baxter Boys. Sid so lovingly referred to those who had grown up under his ministry and had themselves gone into the ministry as the Baxter Boys. What a privilege that would have been!
>
> I only got to know him well in the last five years of his life. Before that, I had heard him preach and had marveled at his use of the English language, the careful cadence and control of his baritone voice, the faithful exposition of scripture and, always as he spoke, the purposeful pointing of men and women to his glorious Savior, Jesus Christ. I had heard his radio program where he was required to condense his devotional message. It must have been hard for him, when he was so pleased to talk long and often about his Lord.

210

The death of a mutual friend was what became, for me, the introduction needed to provide opportunity for visits and for spending time together talking about the things of God. If Sid knew I was speaking today, he would probably, like all good Baptist preachers I know, require me to have three points to the remarks I want to make. And so I shall.

Number one. J. Sidlow Baxter was a prayerful man. You couldn't be in his presence very long until you knew he "had been with Jesus." He knew the blessing of faith-believing prayer in the same way George Mueller knew it. He recognized the source of power for living, for preaching, for writing and for ministering to the needs of his flock, just as E. M. Bounds knew it. He had learned from his Lord Jesus that prayer was the only way to have a relationship with his Heavenly Father. When he prayed, he relished his prayer time. It took a while for me to learn that, when together we prayed, the prayer time was not to be hurried. At first I was afraid that I would weary him. My prayers were not long. Sid made up for what he must have considered an affront to our Heavenly Father. He would pick up where I left off and, with practiced perfection and decorum, he would add at least twenty minutes to our prayer time.

He loved good food. He was a good eater who ate well. And he relished every bite and morsel. But more . . . he relished with great delight what he had first learned at his mother's knee. J. Sidlow Baxter was a prayerful man.

Number two. J. Sidlow Baxter was a powerful man. It has been said that "the pen is mightier than the sword." It's mightier than the computer, too. A prodigious, productive, prolific writer, he had laid down his pen more than twenty-seven times when manuscripts were completed and more than four hundred times after hymns had been composed. They, like his sermons, have moved thousands of people toward the Savior he so dearly loved. He was a powerful man . . . a man made powerful by the One who had given him the ability to declare God's great glory and marvelous

grace. The power he knew and that others perceived was not of his doing. The God whom he loved entrusted him with gifts few men would ever know how to use.

In a visit with him just a couple of months ago, Sid talked in a way I'd never heard him speak before. We had exchanged greetings. In the next hour I would be his audience. He began, "I have never been a fighter." (He paused). He repeated it, "I have never been a fighter." (He paused again and seemed to be reliving something very real). He continued, "But when someone picked a fight with me, I fought for all I was worth. When I was a child, my dear, precious mother would say to me, 'Jimmy Siddie Backie, never be a fighter, but if you have to fight, if someone else picks a fight with you, fight for all you're worth.'"

He didn't finish his story in the way I'll finish it today. We all know he could have repeated the words that Paul wrote so long ago when he wrote to Timothy: "I have fought the good fight, I have finished the race. I have kept the faith. Now there is in store for me the crown of righteousness which the Lord, the righteous Judge, will award to me on that day—and not only to me, but also to all who have longed for His appearing."

Number three. J. Sidlow Baxter was a prayerful man. The last time I would see him in this life was in the hospital on the Sunday before Christmas. He was very ill, but still gracious; very weak, but still able to give thanks. After a time together, I prayed . . . a longer prayer than months and years before. I had learned. When I had finished praying, he knew it was his turn. He lifted his eyes heavenward and began, "Dear Father . . ." And it was all he was able to say because he was so weak. Of all the wonderful prayers I had had the privilege to witness, this was the most compelling, the most memorable, the most soul-stirring prayer I had ever heard him pray. In those two words, it seemed to me, he had said it all. They well could have been his last prayer here and his first prayer there.

Denied the privilege of an earthly father from the time he was one year old, he knew his heavenly Father well. He talked to Him very, very often. J. Sidlow Baxter was a prayerful man. He knew his Heavenly Father. And he knew his prayer time was time well spent!

There was another memorial service in Scotland, for Sid had always told Isa, his Scottish sweetheart, "Isa, there is no place on earth as lovely as bonny Scotland! When I die promise me you'll take me there." Isa kept her promise. She flew his remains to Scotland and held a memorial service conducted by Rev. R. Sloan and Rev. S. Horne. And then she laid him to rest in the land he loved so well.

His Widow

At age ninety-seven, Isa Baxter is healthy, vibrant, and a delight to be with. Her keen sense of humor can lighten anyone's mood and she enjoys a good laugh. As the sun rises each day in lovely Santa Barbara, Isa can be found sitting in her living room reading a page from Sid's book *Awake My Heart*. If a friend is discouraged, she will tell a funny story to lift their spirits—she still enjoys ministering to others.

Isa has good friends who look after her. However, to be her friend is a blessing in itself. She is loyal—she will fight for you. She will faithfully pray for you. She is a good listener and the kind of trustworthy friend who enjoys giving much more than she receives. Isa is a loving person. No one can better sum up Isa than her own Sid. And, in his words, we will let him tell about her and his love for her.

Romance Rides In

Twice during Isa's lengthening years romance has invaded. Her first and very manly husband became a casualty of the second world war, but he lingered in a disabling illness for some twenty years during all of which time Isa was his faithful nurse. Her second romance was with myself, and still continues—near twenty years now, in the golden bands of wedlock.

Both of us had suffered bereavement, and both of us had resolved not to marry again; but a higher Mind than ours ruled otherwise. An evolution of significant coincidences became clear pointers to the course we should take, and in 1979 we were united in marriage. Those extraordinary "coincidences" which happily precipitated our union be-

Mrs. J. Sidlow Baxter (Isa) and E. A. Johnston

come even more fascinating in retrospect, but in this brief monograph I must leave them locked in secrecy. They would make a glowing chapter in some love novel. Yes, truth is sometimes stranger than fiction. Yes, Isa,

> This is a special day, dear,
> I just can't begin to say
> How very much I love you
> Today and every day. . . .
> How much I wish you happiness,
> Heav'n's best throughout your life,

215

How much it means to share the years
With you, my precious wife.

Ninetieth Birthday of Her Majesty, Queen Isa

This is a great occasion, not the kind that hits the headlines or gets reported by television newscasts. None the less it is an outstanding event; a notable landmark in the pilgrimage of a remarkable person.

Ninety years ago, in a scenic, rural farmland edging Scotland's Cromarty Firth and peeping out across Britain's North Sea, a dinky little baby girl came to planet earth and commenced a life full of episodes. She came in with the usual cry of the new-born, but somehow it had a subtle laughter in it; and that innate pleasant humour sang out through all her years with us—and still does.

As she grew into girlhood and womanhood she was unusually attractive by her beauty and sturdiness, also by an irrepressible humour which communicated cheer to many who were sad-hearted.

In the little town of Invergordon she became a prominent personality, the chair-woman of this, and the secretary of that, and the founder of the "League of Friends", a women's group who gave help at the local hospital, also the innovator of a group who sang hymns at the hospital on Sundays there and brought cheer to the patients. She was always in demand, and always ready. Her benevolent exploits would make an intriguing novel. Do you wonder that I call this a "great occasion"? She is ninety today![1]

216

Isa Baxter at age ninety-seven

fifteen

THE LEGACY

Ye have not chosen me, but I have chosen you, and ordained you, that ye should go and bring forth fruit, and that your fruit should remain: that whatsoever ye shall ask of the Father in my name, he may give it you.

JOHN 15:16

His Friends

If Sid was your friend, he was your friend for life. He was loyal. His circle of friends was collectively blessed because they knew him. They each felt it was an honor to be called his friend. The following letters are tributes from those who knew him.

The first letter is from one of the "Baxter Boys," Rev. Dr. Arthur Paterson Lee of Ontario, Canada. Dr. Lee is a renowned author and lecturer.

It was my privilege to have been baptized by Sid on March 26, 1944, after which I was received into the membership of Charlotte Baptist Chapel in Edinburgh, Scotland.

Dr. Baxter excelled as an expository preacher, a prolific writer, and, as I personally discovered, a very caring pastor. Though the senior minister of a large church he would personally counsel people who had made their decision to accept the Savior, he would visit the sick and he would comfort the bereaved.

I well remember the walks and the talks we had together when he discovered that I wanted to prepare for the ministry. During his time in Edinburgh scores of young men and women responded to God's call to full time service. At one point in time as many as five "Chapel boys" were attending New College, U. of E., two of whom became leaders of the Baptist denomination in Scotland, one a theological principal in Canada, two who became pastors in New Zealand and another a pastor in the United States. These were Peter Barber, Andrew MacRae, Walter Long, Angus MacLeod, and Arthur Lee.

Such were the congregational attendances prior to, and after World War II, that the Chapel's evening services had to be held in the three thousand seat auditorium known as the famous Usher Hall. His ministry was keenly sought after by other churches, Bible conferences and colleges in the U.K., Canada, the United States and elsewhere. On one occasion when invited by Principal E. F. Kevan of the London Bible College, his witty humour showed itself as he thanked the Principal for the invitation to come to "the kingdom of Kevan"!

He had a charming and gracious personality, and he handled the Word of God with great insight and reverence. His interests were global as was his concern for the lost. He visited many mission stations abroad. He was a powerful missionary-minded pastor, and at prayer meetings he would spell out precise details of the needs of the members of the church's missionary family. In those days Charlotte Chapel would have a well-attended Monday prayer meeting in the lecture hall, and on Thursdays a weekly Bible Study conducted in the main sanctuary with hundreds of eager believers with their open Bibles and notebooks. He would often delight us by going to the piano where he would play hymns to tunes of his own composition. During the war years, when the church gave hospitality to visiting soldiers, sailors and airmen, Sid's gifted music ministry would delight servicemen and women far from their home towns.

In two of the churches I pastored here in North America, we were privileged to have in each a week's Deeper Life ministry with JSB. These were Calvary Church in Toronto and Tremont Temple in Boston, Massachusetts. As a board member of World Vision (Canada), I rejoiced when he was invited to bring the Devotional Messages to the international Council held that year in California. This happened in the eighties, and my last recollection of Sid was when he and his dear wife, Isa, entertained me in their home in Santa Barbara in the late nineties. As I entered their car to be driven to the airport he stood, paused then said to me "Arthur, I am just longing to see His face!" If only I had had the presence of mind to have said, "So many of us have seen the radiance of Christ in your face"; and this would have been no exaggeration. Heraldine, my wife, and I thank God upon every remembrance of our favourite pastor. Both of us are fortunate to have been acquainted with Ethel, Sid's first wife, and with Isa, who gave him such wonderful support in his advanced years. Both ladies were faithful and most dedicated wives.

In the sweet bond of Calvary's love,
Arthur Lee

The next letter is from Dr. John C. Schmidt, M.D. of Yorba Linda, California. Dr. John is now the proud owner of Sid's piano.

I am a family physician. I was an elder in our church and had taught various Sunday School classes over the years. In

1982 I was asked to teach a class called "Through the Bible in One Year." I was a great lover of the Word and was spiritually challenged to accept this assignment. I soon felt greatly inadequate to try to teach each book in one hour a week. Even though I got up at 4 a.m. and searched through books, concordances, Bible dictionaries, etc., I still felt inadequate in summarizing the great principles of each book.

About the time I reached the Book of Psalms, a patient of mine came in to my office who was a Baptist minister. I shared my frustration with him, and he said "Oh John, just go find J. Sidlow Baxter's *Explore the Book* and your troubles will vanish!" On the same day my wife found the book at a Christian bookstore. When I began to read it, I thought I was lifted "to the gates of Heaven!" No other book extracts the great principles and major teachings of each book of the Bible. Since then, I've read it with the Bible annually.

In my great gratitude, I called Dr. Sid, who lived in Santa Barbara, about 100 miles from our home, just to thank him for the gift of his book. That was the beginning of an enduring friendship that continued until his departure to be with the Lord. How I looked forward to our visits with him and Isa over the last 20 years. To listen to him share his thoughts and insights on scriptures, to hear him play his piano and many hymns he composed, to enjoy his incredible sense of humor—we felt so blessed to know this wonderful man of faith. He was like a father to me.

I am confident that his *Explore the Book*, as well as his numerous other writings, will nourish the hearts of many until our Lord returns.

The following letter is from Dr. T. C. Danson Smith, Th.D., Litt.D., F.M.E., partner in B. McCall Barbour, publisher of Christian literature in Edinburgh, Scotland.

Rev. J. Sidlow Baxter was called to Charlotte Chapel—an independent Baptist church—in Edinburgh where he ministered for about 18 years. It was a great ministry, sadly interrupted by the 2nd World War. He felt that Revival was about to break out as hundreds attended his Prayer Meetings, but when the men went to war, the women were partly involved in war work at home and numbers fell away.

He organised a team of workers after the war to put a gospel tract in every house in Edinburgh once a month. He also took the city's largest concert hall sometimes in the winter months for a Sunday Evening gospel rally. One lady who heard him there phoned from the railway station and said she was about to board a train but wanted to be a Christian. He replied, "God is still on the phone" and led her to Christ.

He was a great combination of Bible Teacher and Evangelist—something quite unique. Men are usually one or the other.

His writings have helped thousands and his master work EXPLORE THE BOOK is often used in Bible Colleges. This was originally published in six volumes but now is in one very large book.

Towards the end of his ministry in Edinburgh the Lord told him that He had finished with that church as the people were not accepting the Word of God in application to their lives, and so he began an itinerant ministry which lasted over forty years.

As ministers cannot have CLOSE friends (because of jealousy) he had only two men friends in Edinburgh—both elders in his church and they were Mr. James Cossar and Mr. Robert Aitken. They met "on the quiet" for they shared his deeply spiritual life and stood strongly against apostasy and the ecumenical movement.

He must have influenced tens of thousands around the world. Some college in USA or Canada granted him an honorary doctorate.

We trust the above is helpful.

Dr. T. C. Danson Smith

Sid always had an affinity with music ministers who loved hymns and Tanner Riley was no exception. They were good friends and corresponded with one another frequently.

I first met J. Sidlow Baxter in 1978 when he came to Fayetteville, AR for a series of services at University Baptist Church. I was, of course, charmed by his wonderful British accent from the very first. But something much deeper happened as he taught us from the Scriptures. A stirring began in my heart and mind that continues to this day—a hungering to know God and to honor Him as King of my life, and also a deeper love relationship with my Lord Jesus. There also rose up in me a growing appreciation for the ministry of God's Holy Spirit in my total being.

Dr. Baxter quoted freely from his own poetry and from powerful old hymn texts and that drew a delightful response from me as a church musician. To hear him quote a hymn text was second only to hearing him read from God's Word. My, how many a familiar hymn poem took on a fresh significance to me and to many in our congregation! I was privileged to have a number of conversations with Dr. Baxter during this and succeeding visits on the matter of worship and the role of music, particularly hymns. These conversations continue to influence my thinking about church music through the passing of the years.

Dr. Baxter's greatest challenge to my life has been the obvious holiness of life that he exhibited in every contact with him, not just the words of his preaching about the subject. He challenged me to seek that holiness and fullness of God's presence in my own life more than any other person ever has. The reverence and tender love for our Lord that permeated every sermon he preached continues to make me thirst for that relationship to this very moment.

As I have studied his books over these years he continues to challenge my life in so many areas of spiritual understanding and growth. His over-arching grasp of the Bible continually amazes me. *Rethinking Our Priorities* has been

especially stimulating and challenging. His volumes on the
Holy Spirit's work in us have been so wonderfully helpful.
Awake My Heart has set my heart to soaring and singing
for a whole year on more than one reading.

When I remember J. Sidlow Baxter now my heart over-
flows with gratitude to God for his beautiful example of
a faith in God lived out for so many years. He preached
God's Word faithfully, but he also set a marvelous example
of living out what he preached on a daily basis, and my life
is so much richer and fuller because of that. Hallelujah! To
quote my beloved mentor, "Pardon me, was I shouting?"

F. Tanner Riley
Retired Minister of Music
Fayetteville, AR

There are many members of Charlotte Baptist Chapel
who can relate wonderful stories and experiences of their
pastor. Many were saved under his ministry there. One such
member is Irene Hay.

In September of 1998 my husband and I embarked on a
tour of the West Coast of America which had to include
Santa Barbara—the home of Dr. J. Sidlow Baxter. What
a welcome! Gracious, kindly and Godly Dr. Baxter was
overjoyed to see us. "Sid" was just overwhelmed that we
had taken the time to see him.

On that September afternoon I had the privilege of
thanking him for his influence on my life as I grew up
and for the part he played in my conversion. One Sunday
evening as a child of 7 years in Charlotte Chapel the Holy
Spirit touched my heart through Dr. Baxter's preaching on
Revelation 3:20—"Behold I stand at the door and knock",
and I gave my life to Christ.

Dr. Baxter told me that Revelation 3:20 was a favour-
ite text of his and told us the following story: Charlotte
Chapel held Open Air Services at The Mound, Princes
Street, Edinburgh. Many people spoke at The Mound—a

Speaker's Corner. One man, in particular, was disturbed by the Gospel singing and preaching and he spoke to Dr. Baxter asking him to tone down the singing and preaching as it was affecting his communist meetings. For 5 years Sidlow Baxter spoke to this man at least once a week and invited him to Charlotte Chapel. He always said, "you will not get me inside the Church". At the end of 5 years on an especially difficult Open Air, Dr. Baxter made an appeal from Revelation 3:20—"Will anyone open their heart's door to Jesus Christ?" A loud voice cried, "I will"—it was the communist speaker. When they spoke together the communist said he would be at Charlotte Chapel the next Sunday—and he was there! Dr. Baxter said "You see that was what made it all worthwhile—the winning of precious souls for the Lord and it does not happen in a day."

We spoke of the great blessings, large number of conversions and people being called to the Mission Field and Pastoral Ministry during his time at Charlotte Chapel. Dr. Baxter said, "(1) The Holy Spirit moved in power. (2) I was the instrument, the Preacher. (3) Behind me was a praying and committed church membership."

Next we spoke of Summer Services in the Usher Hall in Edinburgh and the many who came to faith in Christ at these services. Again he said it was all the work of the Holy Spirit, with himself the Preacher and a wonderfully committed choir.

I asked about sermons because he had great titles, ex., "The Three Greatest Preachers in the World". He explained he used headings for his sermons but never had a full sermon laid out—one must always be led by the Holy Spirit. The greatest sermons were when he went into the pulpit with a sermon and the Holy Spirit did not allow him to use it—something else was laid on his heart which he was compelled to preach.

He was an inspiring preacher to sit under—his knowledge of language was immense as was his Biblical knowledge and more generally he expanded our minds with details of Plato, Aristotle, Socrates, Confucius and the various religions of the world.

Dr. Baxter was born in Sydney, Australia and came to live in Ashton-under-Lyne now part of Greater Manchester, England. His father left his mother and she brought up the family on her own.

On asking what influenced his life most, he replied, "Three ladies.

(1) My Godly mother who worked as a prison visitor as well as bringing up her family—'I worshiped her'.

(2) My first wife Ethel, the perfect Pastor's wife—gracious, kindly, caring, a woman of prayer.

(3) My second wife Isa with whom 'I shared my latter years'. She is kindly, caring—a very wonderful lady."

My outstanding memory was that he always spoke well of women—never a snide comment came from his lips.

He trained as an accountant, played in a band before studying for the ministry at Spurgeon's College. All these experiences and training were used in his three pastorates—Northampton, Sunderland, and Edinburgh. He always liked the Treasurer of his church to keep him informed of the state of the church finances. He wrote hymns (words and music) one year on the Sunday School Anniversary, the children's choir at Charlotte Chapel used Dr. Baxter's hymn book.

My memory of him is of a man full of the joy of the Lord, gracious, kindly and above all else a Christian Gentleman. On leaving his home at Santa Barbara I said to him, "Paul sat at the feet of Gamaliel, but I sat at the feet of one greater than Gamaliel—Dr. Sidlow Baxter."

I will finish this article with the words of one of Dr. Baxter's poems—

Could deeper, higher wonder ever be?
That He, creation's King, for love of me

226

Once left His throne, ineffable, and came
To hang upon a felon's cross of shame!

Oh thorn-crowned Saviour-King whom I adore
Find in my heart an ever-open door,
Make now my will a highway for Thine own,
Let all my days fulfil Thy will alone.

Warmest Christian Greetings,
Irene Hay
Scotland

Carl and Dorothy Schuele were the owners of a radio station in California that hosted a radio program by J. Sidlow Baxter. Sid's radio ministry was a joy to his heart. Dorothy Schuele speaks of her memories of Sid.

Memories of J. Sidlow Baxter . . .
My husband, Carl,* and I met Dr. Baxter when he was doing a series of talks at Trinity Baptist Church here in Santa Barbara. We were awed by his teaching.

At the time, late 70s, early 80s, we owned a radio station, KRUZ-FM, which was a secular, easy listening, commercial station and were developing a Sunday morning program that would fit in with our regular programming in the hope of reaching the ears of a listener with a Christian message. The idea was to have lovely Christian music for the quarter hour and then for the commercial break, a devotional message done by different Christian spokespersons.

We sought out Dr. Baxter and spoke with him about being one of those spokespersons. At first, he was not interested in doing this, but my husband persevered. Carl prevailed upon him to write out these one-minute nuggets and then to voice them. The program was entitled, "Awake My Heart" after Dr. Baxter's devotional book and went on the air Sunday mornings from 6am to 9am. This program aired on KRUZ until the station was sold in 1996.

227

Thousands of people heard Dr. Baxter's nuggets and were enriched by them.

Through the years we enjoyed the friendship of Dr. Baxter and Isa. There were times of profound conversation, but, also times of fun and laughter. He was truly a blessed servant of God and a blessing to so many.

Dorothy Schuele

*My husband predeceased Dr. Baxter by five or so years. Dr. Baxter was one of the speakers at his funeral.

The members of Charlotte Chapel who were blessed by Dr. Baxter's ministry there still speak fondly of him. Another such member is Mrs. Margaret Addison.

I feel very privileged to write my memories of the late Dr. J. Sidlow Baxter. His ministry was a great blessing to me, and still is in my heart. I came to hear him minister in Charlotte Baptist Chapel Edinburgh in 1937, the year I was saved by the grace of God, at the age of 16 years. I became a member there, after being baptised by Rev. J. Sidlow Baxter. Such a ministry of preaching and teaching was so powerful, and added to my growing in grace, and the knowledge of God's word.

He had a Bible class every Thursday evening in the church hall. I came from these lectures so overwhelmed by the exposition of God's word. Also to hear him playing so professionally on the piano using "Alexander Hymns", as well as his own hymns of words and music, such as "My heart cries out for thee, My Saviour crucified" and "Blessed Holy Spirit, Heaven imparted seal."

The special "Youth For Christ" campaigns held in The Usher Hall, Edinburgh as well as open-air meetings at the Ross Bandstand in West Princes Street Gardens, Edinburgh on Sunday afternoons were such a blessing truly he was fully dedicated to his Lord and Saviour Jesus Christ.

As I said at the beginning I feel so privileged at having this opportunity of relating all I remember of God's servant

Dr. J. Sidlow Baxter, I was able to sit under his ministry until 1953 when he left Charlotte Baptist Chapel Edinburgh to go to America. Our loss was America's gain.
Amen!
Mrs. Margaret Addison
Inverness-shire, Scotland

Blessed are the individuals who were baptized by Dr. Baxter. One such lady is Elsie Lucas from Scotland.

Memories of Rev. Sidlow Baxter:
In June 1941, (at 24 years old) I left my parental home in Oldham, Lancashire, England, to take up a post in HM stationary office, Edinburgh—the beautiful capital city of Scotland. One of my colleagues and his wife were members of Charlotte Baptist Chapel where the Rev. Sidlow Baxter was minister. At that time, I had not the faintest understanding of what it meant to be "converted" or "born again", although as a baby I was baptized in a Congregational church and later confirmed in a Church of England.

One Sunday morning I was taken to C.C. to hear Mr. Baxter. After the service, over lunch, my friends asked, "What did you think of our minister?" My reply was, "I didn't understand much of what he said, but I felt that he is a man who knows God, and I believe that what he said is true."

On 28 December 1941, after the evening service in C.C. I committed my life to Jesus Christ, although the speaker that night was Albert Long who at that time was Scottish Secretary for the Open Air Mission.

One beautiful June evening in 1942, I was baptized by Mr. Baxter in C.C. Since then, God has directed me along many varied ways and to far-away places, but I always thank Him for the foundation of solid Bible teaching presented powerfully interestingly by Sidlow Baxter—and, of course, he, too, came from Lancashire!
Elsie Lucas
Scotland

The people of Santa Barbara who knew Sid were grateful for his ministry there. He touched their hearts in many ways. One whose heart he touched is Mrs. Marjorie Teats.

I first knew Dr. Baxter when he came to preach at Trinity Baptist Church of Santa Barbara, California. We were all impressed by the truth and sincerity of his knowledge of God's Bible. I've been a member there since 1966. I was a discussion leader in Bible Study Fellowship for 20 years. We covered many books of the Bible, but since I've read Dr. Baxter's *Explore the Book* and *Awake My Heart* (my favorite devotional for many years), I have learned so much more from all his books.

I have been a friend of the Baxter's for many years—visiting them and hearing what a wonderful pianist he was. Isa is my dear friend and I love her as family.

Once when I was visiting them some time before he died, as I was getting ready to leave he said to me, "Sit down! I want to pray for you." It was so special—I was about in tears. I will always remember that as long as I live, even though I am 80 years old now.

Sincerely,
Mrs. Marjorie Teats

Now from across the pond, another member of Charlotte Chapel, Eric Smith.

I am an elder at Charlotte Chapel, and although my wife and I have only been members since 1970, I had the privilege of sitting under Mr. Baxter's ministry at Charlotte Chapel, as a teenager (and in my early 20s) from about 1943 to 1953. Sidlow Baxter had a profound influence on my early Christian life, and I have read and re-read his books. (I am in the process of re-reading the early chapters of *Explore the Book*). I have also a number of tapes and find them of immense help and encouragement.

With kind regards and prayerful best wishes.
Yours very sincerely,
Eric and Doreen Smith

Sid touched the hearts of many in California; here is a letter from a man who met Dr. Baxter for the first time at Sid's ninetieth birthday party!

It's truly an honor to memorialize Sidlow. I first met Sidlow at his 90th birthday party. My wife, Mary, had met him prior through his wife, Isa. First impressions are most important and I will never forget our first meeting. Sidlow was a staunch man with a very firm and friendly handshake. As we shook hands in greeting he held my right hand with both his hands as if we were old friends. That was the first time any man had ever shook my one hand with both his and I recall how comfortable and joyful this very proper man made me feel, not to mention his ever present smile. When Sidlow spoke, no matter what the subject, there was always thought, conviction and a smile behind every word. It was immediately obvious upon our first meeting that this man had a deep and reverent love for the Lord. This love was reflected in his love for his precious wife, Isa. The love, respect and gentleness this man showed towards his wife is a rare quality today.

We knew Sidlow for only a few short years, but in that time it was quite apparent to us that this man was first and foremost fully committed to the Lord and expressed the love of Jesus to all those who knew him. Sidlow Baxter, simply put, was the godliest man we have ever known and the impression he left on us was a deep, emotional and spiritual love of our Lord as well as one and other. He was rock solid in his commitment to God and we know that he has a very special place in heaven.

I doubt I will ever meet a man so compassionate and convicted, so loving and kind, so gentle and virtuous as Dr. James Sidlow Baxter. I love this man and we who knew

231

him were truly blessed to be in his presence. Thank you for your time and efforts to honor Sidlow Baxter.

Sincerely in the Lord,
Joe and Mary Fackler
Ventura, California

And now another letter from one in Edinburgh who was a Charlotte Chapel member and a family friend who spent time often in the Baxter home.

I have been asked to tell you of my memories of the Reverend Sidlow Baxter, known to the younger members and friends in C.C. as "J.S.B." Of Mr. Baxter my memories are firstly of a godly man who knew his Lord and walked with Him. He was a gentleman, humble charming and gifted.

I grew up in C.C. during his ministry and have never ceased to thank the Lord for that. All I have known about the scriptures and about a prayer life I learn't sitting at feet, as Mary in Bethany sat and loved the teaching of Jesus, at least I sat "in the pews". J.S.B. was a gifted preacher and Thursday evening at the Bible School was an experience, sadly I have never heard since in the chapel, we were fed and encouraged through his ministry.

J.S.B. was a gifted musician, writer, and a man of great wit. His Miriam and I were of an age we paired up and were buddies. So I was often in their home, how gracious to me were Mr. Baxter and his beloved wife Ethel. To go into their home the Spirit of peace and love permeated throughout. Sadly, after Miriam went to the U.S.A., we lost touch with each other. So often I think of that home and the joy there. My one regret is that I have not been able to contact "Mim" and so often think of her.

When different things arise in the press I still say to my husband, "J.S.B. would have prayed and written what the Bible's answer would be in the different situation." The world has lost a giant when J.S.B. went to heaven, a light went out here, oh that men of his teaching and his love of the Lord would stand up and take his place.

But the Lord was kind and gracious to me, that I lived during his ministry and like a sponge soaked in his teaching and it has carried me on through the years.

J.S.B. was a godly man who loved and served his Lord and was loved by many who had the joy of knowing him.

Yours in our Saviour's love,
Vera Alexander
Edinburgh

When Sid was in his eighties, he would still travel to Scotland and preach in the churches there. Here is a letter from one who heard him at her church.

It is with pride and gratification that I have been asked by Mrs. Isabella Baxter to write a few words about the visit of her late husband, Dr. J. Sidlow Baxter, to preach in the Church of Scotland, Invergordon, a church of which Mrs. Baxter, my husband and myself were members.

It was with great pleasure that we welcomed a visit from this distinguished preacher. He fulfilled in every way to a crowded church every expectation we had had. In simple and impressive words he conveyed to the congregation his interpretation of the word of God. Words which will be remembered always.

Mrs. W. F. Paterson
Tomich, Invergordon, Scotland

Senior members of Charlotte Chapel such as Angus M. Ferguson and Robert White sent a word as well. Here are a few lines in their words:

I have been in Charlotte Baptist Chapel all the 70 years of my life. I remember Sidlow Baxter from when I was a

233

child in the 1930s until the time he left and had personal dealings with him from time to time. He both baptised me and received me into membership of the church. Sidlow Baxter had a striking appearance. Tall, well-set, with a mane of fine hair. He was quiet and dignified and a charmer in conversation. In the pulpit he was an extrovert and flamboyant, serious and authoritative—a mixture. His hearers never quite knew what to expect next! Underneath lay a sense of humor which was almost boyish. He spoke out against the sins of the world and was unafraid to comment forcefully on politics and the world situation. He targeted worldliness in Christians, often entering into details as to what Christians should and should not do; causing controversy. Not everyone was comfortable with this aspect of his preaching. He had a tremendous mastery of scripture. Pastorally, he visited when there were difficulties or an illness. He visited my home twice during the Second World War when my father was in the Royal Air Force and my mother was in a difficult situation with family illness. Once while visiting my mother in the hospital, he spoke with her and then prayed. On his way out of the ward, he stopped and asked all the lady patients if they would like him to pray for them and their relatives at home. They willingly agreed and everyone in the ward stopped to listen while he prayed—it made a great impression.

Yours sincerely,

Angus M. Ferguson

From a history of Charlotte Chapel (now out of print) of which I have a copy I can say that Mr. Baxter commenced his pastorate in October 1935 and continued until 1953. During this ministry I was indebted to him with my wife when he conducted our wedding in 1940. I trust you will have success and find the help you need.

Yours in our shared Eternal Faith,

Robert White (Robin among friends)

One of the last friends Sid had was Benton L. Tibbetts. Here are some of his recollections:

Although I am a scientist (geophysicist) by profession, I have long been a student of the Bible. When J. Sidlow Baxter's *Explore the Book* fell into my hands in the Spring of 1988, I struck gold! Sid shared many wonderful experiences with me over the short two years that I was privileged to know him. Sid would occasionally sit at his Steinway piano and give me marvelous mini-concerts. He wrote over a hundred hymns. He was without a doubt the most multi-gifted person I have ever been privileged to know, let alone have him call me his friend. A few weeks before he was struck with the influenza that would eventually take his life, he remarked to me one day, "Benton, I think I shall reach a hundred." Retirement did not come easy to Sid. He was not always happy. He often complained that he was not doing anything for the Lord. I would then remind him as forcefully as I could about the good his thirty-odd books were doing, and that on my own nightstand there rested two masterpieces: my Bible and *Explore the Book*. I read both every day. Sid would lift his head in his own inimitable way and intone; "Ah, Benton, you are such an encouragement." I miss him!

Born in Australia, J. Sidlow Baxter always maintained deep friendships with people there. One such person was the Reverend T. Douglas Carty. Rev. Carty played a special role in Sid's book *The Hidden Hand*, for it was he who was the stolen baby in the book. He sent the following letter to Isa immediately after Dr. Baxter's death.

The man God made long ago has now farewelled into God's Own Home. His sermons are on audio tapes and in his many magnificent books in most of this world's nations. Gratitude for him and love to him beats in many hearts and memories everywhere he has been. Wealthy in scriptures and rich in voice, and greatly empowered in statements about our Lord and Savior Christ Jesus, he will still be effective in our lives.

Happily suited to meet all kinds of people he has been welcomed by the angels, and now his great love for real music will now be satisfied in its greatest heights. We who keenly miss his quiet yet dynamic personality are applauding this delightful apostle's expressions of faith in his guiding Lord. Expressions which have heightened our faith in the crucified, resurrected, ascended only Son of God.

The writer of these words is unable to express just what he feels for grand fellowship with this man who has been a powerful effect, by so many means, in so many times, on him. Thank you Lord, for my dear friend Sidlow.

T. Douglas Carty
Wyee, Australia

POSTSCRIPT

The great golfer Ben Hogan intimated that he possessed "a secret" to his flawless golf swing. The golfing world tried unsuccessfully to pry that secret out of him—he never divulged it and supposedly it died with him. J. Sidlow Baxter had a secret to living the Christian life, but unlike Ben Hogan, he was willing to share it with others. Near the end of Dr. Baxter's ministry, he divulged a fourfold formula or "secret" for living a victorious Christian life. What Dr. Baxter related is the following:

1. What I give to Him He takes
2. What He takes He cleanses
3. What He cleanses He fills
4. What He fills He uses[1]

F. B. Meyer once remarked, "I have known men when you meet them it is evident that Christ was present. For to be saved the scripture says, 'But if any man hath not the Spirit of Christ, he is none of his.' So if a man is a Christian then Christ is present. Then I have known other men, though not

as many, where Christ was not only *present* but *prominent.*
Then sadly, I have known fewer still, where Christ was not
only *present and prominent but also preeminent.*"[2]

Since F. B. Meyer knew J. Sidlow Baxter, it wouldn't be
surprising to learn that perhaps he was speaking of him.
Adrian Rogers once said that being in the presence of
J. Sidlow Baxter was like being in the presence of Jesus.
Sidlow Baxter had his faults. He was tightfisted with his
money, he was hard-headed at times, and he had trouble
forgiving his daughter. All in all he was human, yet he lived
a consecrated life with a heavenly focus.

J. Sidlow Baxter left us a legacy. His keen insights into
Holy Writ, his talents as a writer, his ability as a preacher,
and his Christlike example of a sanctified life should be
a clarion call to those of us who desire to live a holy life,
pleasing to the Lord. He was a man who possessed a duality
of life in that while he lived in the mortal flesh, his mind
stayed in heaven; he spent his time here on this orb as one
whose heart was truly awake to his Lord.

AFTERWORD

NO PAINTED STICKS

I first heard the name J. Sidlow Baxter in 1964. A friend gave me a copy of Sidlow's book *Awake My Heart*. Although I knew nothing of the man, the words of his pen began to plant an indelible impression. He recounts the story of watching a caterpillar move through the English grass seeking sustenance. A croquet set had been used the previous evening and the painted sticks were still in place. The caterpillar approached the first stick, climbed to the top, raised up on his tiny "feet" seeking the juicy leaves, but discovered nothing was there! He climbed down, moved further along the ground and encountered the second stick. This one also was climbed and the futile exercise was repeated. He finally climbed down again with nothing to sustain or strengthen him. Our beloved Sidlow mused to himself of the perfect picture before him of fallen man seeking life! The sons of Adam climb thousands of "painted sticks," find nothing, and start the empty process all over. It is only when we climb "the tree of life" offered by the Savior . . . rather than the "sticks painted by men" . . . that we find the nourishment, illumination, and confidence of our Lord's inexhaustible

239

feast of truth. Our lives then begin to soar with significance, strength, and satisfaction!

Sidlow Baxter was one of the few I have known who saw to it that he climbed the minimum of "painted sticks." This must be the reason the Lord Jesus was not only present and prominent in his life but clearly *preeminent*. Little did I dream that the author of *Awake My Heart* would, some ten years later, become my deepest and most intimate friend for over twenty-five years. Through the Lord's sovereign initiative, I was prompted to invite him to preach at the church I pastored in the fall of 1974. From that first meeting a bond developed which increased over the years until his final, joyful departure to see the Savior.

That Sidlow stood out in a crowd would be an understatement. At over six feet tall, with flowing white hair, a dignity of presence and posture, and an unusual glow about his face, you knew instantly that a unique individual confronted you. It was confirmed with absolute confidence once he opened his mouth! Even the most casual, trivial, mundane issue evoked from him perfect wording, precise inflection, and penetrating diction. Every issue was brightened by the incredible breadth of his vocabulary. After initial greetings at the airport and finally seating ourselves in my car, his first words were, "Tell me, what does H. D. stand for?" I replied, "Harvey Dwight." Then, before I could begin to explain the origin of the names, he quickly said, "Ahhh, Harvey! That's a good English name! I'll call you that." Hence, the only person on earth who called me Harvey McCarty was J. Sidlow Baxter. He expressed himself so positively that every time he spoke my name, I felt a fresh surge of strength and pride.

In the following twenty-five years of our earthly fellowship, Sid spoke more at our church than at any place else on earth other than his three pastorates in England! His last speaking tour in America came in the summer of 1991 at age eighty-eight. He spoke for his dear friend, Charles Blair, in Denver, Colorado, then went to our mutual friend Adrian Rogers in Memphis, Tennessee, and finally came to us, enduring what his beloved Isa said was "their worst plane trip ever." (It was a terrible day for turbulence!) Sid never mentioned the discomfort to the church!

Although we had enjoyed their home on earlier occasions, from 1992 on, my wife and I visited the Baxters annually for his birthday celebration. We will never forget those delightful and inspiring journeys to beautiful Santa Barbara, the lunches, afternoon teas, the drives, and dinners together and above all, the invigorating and creative reflections on the Lord Jesus that flowed through Sidlow's mind and heart until his last days. My only apprehensions were over the amount he tipped the waiters when it was his turn. He never lost his sense of Scottish frugality! I often added to the tip without him knowing it!

During those final years from the end of his traveling ministry in 1991 to his home going in December 1999, I spoke to him regularly on an almost every-other-week cycle. Some conversations were brief, and others were lengthy. I busied myself taking notes on every conversation. Even his casual comments and simple observations were loaded with spiritual insight and Biblical liberation. I could write a book on these notes alone as his comments enlightened every issue with a practical grasp of obvious application. Sidlow was truly one of the Lord's choice servants to whom was given a ministry through writing, preaching, and counseling that would touch millions. Even in his nineties he was answering correspondence from all over the world by handwritten responses on spiritual issues! Visiting Charlotte Chapel, Edinburgh, in 1992, I spoke to some of those who profited from his ministry while he was pastor. One lady's testimony summed it up best when she declared, "I asked Pastor Baxter to visit our home, as I was concerned about the unbelief of my husband." As she walked him to the door, she whispered to Sid, "Your presence has changed his mind about the Lord and His church!" to which Sid responded, "If he is changed, then it certainly was not *my* presence but *His*." Although the event was at least forty-three years previous, I still saw the glint of tears in her eyes.

From our first meeting there was an instant deepening of a wonderful friendship. It grew like father and son. (My own father was born in 1904 but killed himself when he was thirty-one.) I have all Sidlow's books, have heard scores of his sermons, have visited his home many times and he mine, known Ethel and Isa, shared several hundred phone calls, and have read and reread my multitudinous notes on his sermons and our conversations for over twenty-five years. He gave me copies of all his unpublished manuscripts and he and Isa gifted me his library, desk, and personal handmade glass bookcase when he died. To the day I conducted his funeral in Santa Barbara in January 2000, I have been a student of J. Sidlow Baxter. Yet his mind was so brilliant and his output so vast I have only skimmed the surface. I confessed at his funeral, "I feel like an ant trying to describe a lion!"

The honor of writing this "afterword" granted me by my friend and author, E. A. Johnston, has forced me to sharpen my focus. I offer seven outstanding qualities of Sidlow's life that reflect on his essence as a lover of Christ. First was his precision. Second was his touch with God. Third was his rare gift of preaching. Fourth, his ability to hear Christ's voice through the apparent weaknesses of others. Fifth, his sense of our common failures that elicited forgiveness rather than judgment. Sixth, his strategic grasp of prayer; and seventh would be his love of great hymns. I will not even mention his incredible ability to see the fullness of Christ in Scripture, his impeccable scholarship, or his powerful use of language and pen. I sense these latter three qualities are but an outgrowth of the other seven.

First, Sidlow was my finest mentor in learning the power of precision. I have come to see that "the deeper life" that most Christians say they hunger for is really nothing more than "the precise life." J. Sidlow Baxter was a master at being precise! Only precision in obeying the Lord Jesus leads to depth on the path of holiness. Sidlow once told me of a young British evangelist who was marvelously gifted as a speaker. Sid encouraged him to write, to which the young man responded most positively.

Months later when Sid ran across him again, he asked about his attempts at writing. The young man responded that it was too wearisome of a task. "Frankly, Brother Baxter, it sometimes takes me a whole hour just to write one paragraph." Sidlow summarized his analysis to me in the following fashion: "I said nothing to him, Harvey, but marveled at his lack of understanding. In my writing it would sometimes take me a whole morning to pen just one sentence." In every area (music, theology, diet, politics, history, Greek, etc.), Sidlow Baxter's life was displayed with precision. No wonder his writing grips the reader with such power. Every phrase is skillfully packed with precision!

In one of many conversations with my beloved Sid in his last year, he queried me with his usual Baxterian thoroughness, "Tell me, Harvey, what is e-mail?" (This was 1999!!!) I explained to him the process, to which he gave his usual thoughtful and briefly delayed response, "Hmmm . . . I am so out of touch with the fancies of this modern age, but then I suppose being out of touch with man's cleverness matters little if I am still *in touch with Him.*" Sidlow seemed to be "in touch" with Christ about every experience, question, or circumstance of his life. This small observation reveals his huge proclivity for seeing the Lord Jesus in everything! This is the second quality that touched me deeply. It seems all his responses to life were God-connected.

A third quality would have to be his preaching. In one of our moments together, he related Metropolitan Tabernacle's overtures for him to become their pastor and stand in Spurgeon's stead in London. The essence was Sidlow's time spent with William Olney Jr., who (like his father) had been Spurgeon's secretary. At the time, Olney was over one hundred years old when Sidlow (at age thirty-five) spoke to him in the late 1930s. (Sid told me that it was well that he did not leave Edinburgh for London, as German bombs destroyed the tabernacle within two years!) In discussing this experience he philosophized, "Harvey, I am not sure why I am telling you this. I have not mentioned it to others, but I asked Mr. Olney why would they want the likes of Sidlow Baxter at the great Metropolitan Tabernacle? Harvey, he answered me that I was more like the Governor than anyone else he had ever heard!" Perhaps, dear readers, Sidlow's quality as a preacher is nothing more than the giftedness of God, which he disciplined himself to develop more fully than most, just like "the Governor." Sid's hold on Christ must have been akin to Spurgeon's! When I listen to Dr. Baxter's tapes, I wonder how close he really was to speaking like the "Prince of Preachers."

Sidlow possessed incredible insight in seeing and hearing Christ in the strengths and weaknesses of others. Hear this fourth quality from his account of a 1921 experience in London:

I remember when I was at Spurgeon's College that a certain Christian leader was invited to speak in chapel. I recall well the subject: "Prayer, Praise, and Preaching." The problem was that our speaker had a strong lisp and simply could not pronounce his "r's." As he stood and read the Scriptures and then announced his subject, all of us chuckled to ourselves at his language difficulties. It was difficult to restrain laughter.

Yet he boldly proclaimed, "Young men, today I wish to speak to you on the subject of 'Pwayer, Pwaise, and Pweaching.'" But, dear Harvey, he preached with such eloquence, such depth, and such anointing of the Spirit, by the time he finished his message, we were all envying him his handicap!

This story, over eighty years after it happened and over twenty years since I first heard it, still stirs and enflames my heart in its retelling. Sid knew how to hear the Savior through others and to pass it on!

The fifth quality was Sid's compassion for and understanding of mankind's mutual fallenness and lostness. I recall this lesson as though it were yesterday. I was driving him to a speaking engagement. In my youthful forties, I was still too quick and guilty of judging other men and their ministries. We were discussing the problem of leadership in the church. One particular charismatic preacher that I had difficulty with came to mind. I sensed Sidlow concurred with me in his own evaluation of the man's ministry and unbalanced approach (at least as I perceived it!).

Although the Spirit checked me before I asked, I still blundered on with a loaded and suggestive question that exposed my prejudice. "Brother Sid," I asked as innocently and piously as possible, "what do you think about so-and-so?" It is one of those questions that can hardly be answered correctly by the immature! I instantly regretted asking it, but it was too late to retract. He pondered a full minute before giving one of the most magnificent responses I have ever heard and that I shall never forget. "Well, Harvey, he is one of us!" Case closed! I must have felt exactly like the Pharisees when Jesus gave them one of his amazing answers to their pointless questions!

The sixth and possibly greatest quality of his life was his passion for prayer. It was truly a two-way conversation between him and his Savior to hear him pray. This illuminating experience makes my point. I arrived at the motel to pick him up for the evening meeting. The door was partially ajar and just as I knocked, I recognized that he and Ethel were in prayer. I apologized profusely for interrupting their prayer time, but he stood to receive me in his usual smiling, gentlemanly fashion and dismissed the interruption. "Oh no, Harvey, it is good to see you! Won't you join us? We were just having a spot of prayer!" Sid and I then sat down, and he continued with these words: "Now, dear Father, as we were saying before Harvey came . . ."

A second beautiful story has to do with prayer and aging. He told me this when he was ninety-five. "When I was seventy-five and sought the Lord's blessing for further usefulness, He told me two things—that if I would stay close to the cross and be careful in my eating, He would give me ten more years. Think of it, Harvey, He has given me twenty!" He was "loaded" on the subject of nutrition!

Perhaps one of his more profound experiences in prayer came when he faced another "old age" crisis at seventy-five. His health was broken, he had just lost his first wife, Ethel, to cancer, and it seemed his ministry was at an end. He recalled lying in bed late at night in his little apartment and talking to the Lord. "I remember telling the Savior, Harvey, with some depth of anguish, that there was nothing left ahead of me. But then his voice came clearly, 'Sid, Sid, I am still ahead of you!' I sat up, my heart was instantly stilled, and I haven't had a moment of self-pity since."

With two-way conversations like that between Sidlow and his Lord . . . continuous, intimate, honest, and earnest . . . is it any wonder that Sidlow's prayers breathed spiritual reality? His interchanges with the Father exceeded those of any person I ever heard pray! He did not pray to impress. People's awe came automatically when they recognized he was truly speaking to his dear Savior. His simple childlike words and the avoidance of the stale, formalized, routine, and usual Christian verbiage made his prayers exciting, fresh, and authentic. The anticipation was always great when we asked Sidlow to lead us in prayer. He talked with the Savior as he talked to us and as though he was seated at his side. I still yearn to pray like that. I can truly feel the heart of the disciples as they asked Jesus to "teach us to pray" . . . like you pray!

One of the most tender illuminations on Sidlow's prayer life must be traced to his dear, beloved mother. Even in his later years, he spoke of her with the affection of a little boy. Her influence on his life was incalculable, as she was raising him alone. "There was hardly a morning, Harvey, when I awoke and went to our little kitchen that I did not see her kneeling next to her bed in prayer." I know that dear lady has had her joys multiplied a millionfold in heaven for the example she set for her little son. I can see Sidlow saying with compassionate earnestness, "Every mommy and daddy should take that observation to heart. No greater agony can be reaped on earth than for parents to realize they failed to point their children toward the Savior. I shall never, ever forget the powerful example of my dear mother in prayer."

The goal of prayer is yieldedness. I once asked my beloved Sid at age ninety-three for the one thing I could pray for him most. He pondered a moment and soberly replied, "Simply pray, Harvey, that I shall be more yielded." This must be the highest purpose and achievement of prayer. Sidlow had learned it well.

Seventh and lastly, Sidlow was a gifted musician, pianist, composer, and arranger. He loved the great music of the church. I have in my study an old English valise with a hymnbook that he personally prepared for publication.

Many of the hymns were written by Sidlow himself; others, uniquely arranged; and others, with different verses freshly composed. Believe it or not, it contains over eight hundred hymns. The title of this hymnbook is *Hymns for Worship and Witness*. I have the only copy in existence. It was his dream to have it published. He told me on several occasions when I explored helping him raise the money for the project that "the cause" would probably be lost. He lamented that so few people today love the great hymns of the faith and that our music so often moves "from dignity to drivel." He grieved over the sad shallowness of American worship . . . especially our music.

Shirley and I still cherish the times of worship in his home when he would play the piano, and we sang the great hymns together. His knowledge of hymnology, his incredible memory, and ability to recall stanzas of multitudes of hymns and great lines from poetry stuns me to this day. He even composed a cantata that we premiered at my church. Sid did the narration, accompanied by orchestra, choir, and soloists. He felt it was one of the greatest gifts our church ever gave him. I must say again I have known none who was a truer master in so many fields.

On what was our final visit to both Sidlow and Isa, Shirley and I asked him to close our hymn time by playing "Like a River Glorious," one of his most favorite hymns. Isa stood with us as we watched him play with great finesse while we sang together. I recall the tear in my eye, knowing it would possibly be the last time I would hear him play and we would sing together on earth. He would consider it a tragic oversight for someone to write a little volume on his life and not mention at least one great hymn. It is obvious why we selected this great text and melody for his funeral. In Sid's honor then, I give you once more the words of the hymn he loved as dearly as any other:

Like a river glorious is God's perfect peace,
Over all victorious in its bright increase;
Perfect, yet it floweth fuller ev'ry day,
Perfect, yet it groweth deeper all the way.

Hidden in the hollow of His blessed hand,
Never foe can follow, never traitor stand;
Not a surge of worry, not a shade of care,
Not a blast of hurry touch the spirit there.

Ev'ry joy or trial falleth from above,
Traced upon our dial by the Sun of Love;
We may trust Him fully all for us to do—
They who trust Him wholly find Him wholly true.

Chorus

Stayed upon Jehovah, hearts are fully blest—
Finding as He promised, perfect peace and rest.

Untold thousands would shout in unison that here was
a man, if there ever was one, "Stayed Upon Jehovah!"

Scores of his insights have restored and sustained me
in the battle. In one of our last phone conversations, he
assured me, "I have no one in America whom I have loved
more than Harvey McCarty. In fact, when I see the Savior,
and it is permissible in his presence, yours will be one of
the first names I call to his attention! You can count on it!"
Sid could capture and bring the creative power of Christ to
one's heart in minutes while it would take most of us hours
. . . if at all! The world still needs to drink richly from the
cup of men like J. Sidlow Baxter.

Another phrase Sid used repeatedly indicates strongly
why God used him in such amazing fashion. "Harvey, I am
truly the Lord's most unworthy and unprofitable servant."
I couldn't believe at first that he really meant this, knowing

the millions of lives touched by Christ through him. Yet as I have grown older and realized my own deeper need of grace; and as I learned Sidlow Baxter's heart and mind more clearly, I am persuaded this was his sincere conviction!

I would suggest this sense of unworthiness and unprofitability gripped him powerfully because he saw the vastness of God's grace and the puniness of our response. On one occasion in his living room, he suddenly declared (out of the blue), "Think of it, Harvey. Every morning the sovereign Lord of the universe deigns to come and meet with Sidlow Baxter in my little study!" These "outbursts of worship" were common in almost every conversation. Another of his favorites, often used was, "What a dear, dear Savior we have!" Such spontaneous expressions evidenced powerfully his own counsel to be "intensely spiritual, perfectly natural, and thoroughly practical."

In our last earthly meeting Sid expressed his sense of sadness that he couldn't return to the preaching ministry and be "back in the fight." (He still found energy to brush up on his Greek at age ninety-five and complete two manuscripts in his nineties!) It was raining heavily; it was a drowsy time after lunch, and his usual vitality had lost some of its edge. As he spoke of his sense of uselessness, I sought to encourage him with thoughts of his outstanding achievements for Christ ... his many books and honors, his international preaching, the multiplied thousands whose lives he had helped change ... including my own ... but as I spoke he interrupted with, "Dear Harvey," bowed his head, closed his eyes, and concluded, "I have done nothing, nothing, nothing!" We sat in silence for several minutes. I knew I had heard the ultimate statement that could be made by one of the Lord's truly anointed. It was no time for me to be one of Job's counselors! I am convinced Sidlow was a close human fulfillment of one of his own finest insights—"A man full of himself cannot preach the Christ *who emptied Himself.*"

Old age held for him no fear! He told me often, "The Lord Jesus is nearer, clearer, and dearer than He has ever been." On several occasions he would indicate "up" and smilingly comment, "I'm more there than here!" He loved to testify, "Old age is wonderful! I wouldn't have missed it for the world! If it were not for this old body and its health problems, it would be our most glorious period of life!" Sid taught me that to be old, healthy, and deeply in Christ is to find the best this earthly life has to offer.

Sid, the proper English gentleman, always wore a tie—even around the house!

Thank you, J. Sidlow Baxter, for all you gave the world of the wonder of the Lord Jesus. And thank you, Sid, for all you were and remain to me. In knowing you could do *nothing*, you became a candidate for *everything* the Savior had for you. No one I have ever known has embraced Christ Jesus more fully . . . and I shall never forget! When we also learn we can do nothing but yield, we too shall live, as the title of this book states, with "a heart awake" to our Lord!

DR. H. D. McCARTY
SENIOR PASTOR OF UNIVERSITY BAPTIST CHURCH
FAYETTEVILLE, ARKANSAS

NOTES

Chapter 1: The Lad

1. J. Sidlow Baxter, *Does God Still Guide?* (Grand Rapids: Zondervan, 1971), 64.

2. J. Sidlow Baxter, *Daily Wings* (Grand Rapids: Zondervan, 1983), 258.

3. J. Sidlow Baxter, *For God So Loved* (Grand Rapids: Kregel, 1995), 30.

4. Baxter, *Does God Still Guide?*, 95.

5. J. Sidlow Baxter, *Going Deeper* (Grand Rapids: Zondervan, 1976), 154.

6. J. Sidlow Baxter, *The Master Theme of the Bible* (Grand Rapids: Kregel, 1997), 143. Hymn lyrics quoted are by Wade Robinson, "I Am His, and He Is Mine." Original copyright in 1890.

Chapter 2: The Young Adult

1. J. Sidlow Baxter, *Majesty, The God You Should Know* (San Bernardino, CA: Here's Life Publishers, 1984), 127–28.

2. Baxter, *Does God Still Guide?*, 47.

3. J. Sidlow Baxter, "Philippians 4:6–7" (taped message, Bellevue Baptist Church, Memphis: Love Worth Finding Ministries, May 19, 1991).

4. J. Sidlow Baxter, *Explore the Book* (Grand Rapids: Zondervan, 1960), 5.

5. J. Sidlow Baxter, "Wembley Reverie," 1921, from the personal papers of Isabella Baxter.

Chapter 3: The Early Marriage

1. J. Sidlow Baxter, *Divine Healing of the Body* (Grand Rapids: Zondervan, 1979), 250.

2. Baxter, *Does God Still Guide?*, 87.

3. J. Sidlow Baxter, "A Sweet Acrostic," July 2, 1923, from the personal papers of Isabella Baxter.

4. J. Sidlow Baxter, *The Hidden Hand* (Wheaton: Living Books Publishers, 1985), 198.

5. Baxter, *Does God Still Guide?*, 64–65.

6. Baxter, *Majesty, The God You Should Know*, 220.

7. J. Sidlow Baxter, "Sympathetic Lines of a Father to a Daughter in Bed with Mumps," undated, between 1930 and 1952, from the personal papers of Isabella Baxter.

8. J. Sidlow Baxter, birthday poem to Miriam, 1977, from the personal papers of Isabella Baxter.

9. J. Sidlow Baxter, "Missing," undated, from the personal papers of Isabella Baxter.

Chapter 4: The Early Pastorates

1. Baxter, *Does God Still Guide?*, 65–66.

2. C. H. Spurgeon, The *Banner of Truth*.

Chapter 5: The Edinburgh Pastorate

1. *Charlotte Chapel Record*, February 1944.

2. W. Graham Scroggie, *A Guide to the Psalms* (Grand Rapids: Kregel, 1995), 145–46.

3. Baxter, *Explore the Book*, 6–9.

4. Ian Balfour, quoted in Rev. William Whyte, *Revival in Rose Street, A History of Charlotte Baptist Chapel* (Edinburgh: Lindsay & Co. Ltd., 1953), 60–61.

5. Keith Skelton, interview with J. Sidlow Baxter, July 1995.

6. J. Sidlow Baxter, "Constant Victory over the Flesh" (taped message, Bellevue Baptist Church, Memphis: Love Worth Finding Ministries, March 1, 1977), used by permission.

7. Baxter, *Does God Still Guide?*, 155–67.

Chapter 6: The Move across the Atlantic

1. C. H. Spurgeon, *The Full Harvest, Volume 2* (Edinburgh: Banner of Truth Trust, 1987), 253.

2. Keith Skelton, interview with J. Sidlow Baxter, July 1995.

3. J. Sidlow Baxter, *Rethinking Our Priorities* (Grand Rapids: Zondervan, 1980), 155.

4. SiteReports, "Demographics," Santa Barbara Region Chamber of Commerce, http://www.sbchamber.org/relocation/demographics.html (accessed January 26, 2004).

Chapter 7: The Illness and the Healing

1. Baxter, *Divine Healing of the Body*, 256–58.

2. Ibid., 250–53.

Chapter 8: The Grief and the Loss

1. Quoted in Baxter, *Divine Healing of the Body*, 259–60.

Chapter 9: The Scottish Sweetheart

1. J. Sidlow Baxter, "Philippians 4:6–7" (taped message, Bellevue Baptist Church, Memphis: Love Worth Finding Ministries, spring 1991).

Chapter 10: The Itinerant Preaching

1. W. Y. Fullerton, *F. B. Meyer, A Biography* (Ontario, Canada: Ontario Christian Books, 1992), 208–9.

2. J. Sidlow Baxter, luncheon meeting (taped message, Bellevue Baptist Church, Memphis: Love Worth Finding Ministries, March 1977).

3. J. Sidlow Baxter, luncheon meeting (taped message, March 1, 1977).

4. J. Sidlow Baxter, "An Octogenarian Testimony" (taped message, University Baptist Church, Fayetteville, AR, 1980s).

Chapter 11: The Author and Poet

1. Adrian Rogers, interview with author, 2002.

2. John Phillips, personal correspondence with author, 2001.

3. Baxter, *Explore the Book*, 9–10.

4. Ibid., 12.

5. Ibid., 101.

6. Ibid., 102.

7. J. Sidlow Baxter, "Love's Gentle Chivalry," 1924 or 1925, from the personal papers of Isabella Baxter.

8. J. Sidlow Baxter, "Tornado! Cruelest, deadliest scare!" undated, from the personal papers of Isabella Baxter.

9. J. Sidlow Baxter, "Operation Morning," August 3, 1936, from the personal papers of Isabella Baxter.

10. J. Sidlow Baxter, "A Love Problem," 1917 or 1928, from the personal papers of Isabella Baxter.

11. J. Sidlow Baxter, *Enter Ye In* (London: Marshall, Morgan & Scott, 1939), 2.

12. Ibid., 12.

13. J. Sidlow Baxter, *Mark These Men* (London: Marshall, Morgan & Scott, 1949), 83.

14. Baxter, *Going Deeper*, 97–100.

15. J. Sidlow Baxter, *Awake My Heart* (Grand Rapids: Kregel, 1994), 45.

16. J. Sidlow Baxter, *Studies in Problem Texts* (Grand Rapids: Zondervan, 1960), 7.

17. Baxter, *For God So Loved*, 4.

18. J. Sidlow Baxter, *A New Call to Holiness* (Grand Rapids: Kregel, 1993), 7.

19. Baxter, *Does God Still Guide?*, 137.

20. Ibid., 43–44.

21. Baxter, *The Master Theme of the Bible*, 9.

22. Baxter, *Rethinking Our Priorities*, 7.

23. Baxter, *Majesty, The God You Should Know*, 7.

24. J. Sidlow Baxter, *The Other Side of Death* (Wheaton: Tyndale, 1987), 5.

25. J. Sidlow Baxter, "HERE we praise the God of grace," unpublished hymn, private papers.

26. J. Sidlow Baxter, "Sanctify me wholly," unpublished hymn, private papers.

Chapter 12: The Octogenarian

1. Joyce Rogers, *The Bible's Seven Secrets to Healthy Eating* (Wheaton: Crossway, 2001), 100.
2. Ibid., 101.
3. Baxter, *Our High Calling*, 157.
4. Baxter, *Divine Healing of the Body*, 255.
5. Baxter, *Our High Calling*, 159–60.
6. Ibid., 169–70.

Chapter 13: The Praying Saint

1. Baxter, *Does God Still Guide?*, 139.
2. Ibid., 140–41.
3. Ibid., 150–51.
4. J. Sidlow Baxter, *A New Call to Holiness* (Grand Rapids: Kregel, 1993), 45–59.
5. Ibid., 46.
6. Ibid., 57.
7. Ibid., 58.
8. Ibid., 59.

Chapter 14: The Heavenly Homecoming

1. From the personal papers of Isabella Baxter.

Postscript

1. J. Sidlow Baxter, "Hints on Prayer" (taped message, University Baptist Church, Fayetteville, AR, 1988).
2. F. B. Meyer, quoted by J. Sidlow Baxter, "The Believer's Sanctification" (taped message, University Baptist Church, Fayetteville, AR, 1978).

E. A. Johnston is a fellow of the Stephen Olford Institute for Biblical Preaching and is actively involved in Bible teaching and disciple making. He has written several books. Dr. Johnston holds four earned degrees in theology from Master's Divinity School in Evansville, Indiana. He lives in Memphis, Tennessee.